DEDICATION

PREFACE

PART I: FOUNDATIONS OF ORGANIZATIONAL DEVELOPMENT

CHAPTER 1: INTRODUCTION TO ORGANIZATIONAL DEVELOPMENT AND CHANGE

CHAPTER 2: CORE CONCEPTS AND APPROACHES IN ORGANIZATIONAL DEVELOPMENT

CHAPTER 3: IMPROVISATION AND ORGANIZATIONAL INNOVATION

CHAPTER 4: ORGANIZATIONAL STRATEGY AND LEARNING

CHAPTER 5: SOCIAL NETWORK ANALYSIS

PART II: ADVANCED CONCEPTS IN MANAGING CHANGE

CHAPTER 6: WHOLE SYSTEMS CHANGE

CHAPTER 7: MICRO-LEVEL CHANGE: TEAM DYNAMICS AND PROCESS IMPROVEMENTS

CHAPTER 8: MINDFULNESS AND STRESS REDUCTION

CHAPTER 9: KNOWLEDGE MANAGEMENT

CHAPTER 10: COLLABORATIVE LEARNING AND TECHNOLOGY STRATEGY

PART III: GLOBAL PERSPECTIVES AND CORPORATE RESPONSIBILITY

CHAPTER 11: GLOBAL LABOR MARKETS

CHAPTER 12: CORPORATE SOCIAL RESPONSIBILITY (CSR)

CHAPTER 13: SOCIAL JUSTICE, DIVERSITY, AND INCLUSION

CHAPTER 14: TRANSFORMATIONAL LEADERSHIP METHODS

PART IV: INNOVATIVE METHODS AND FUTURE DIRECTIONS

CHAPTER 15: SYSTEMS DYNAMICS AND ORGANIZATIONAL DESIGN

CHAPTER 16: APPRECIATIVE INTELLIGENCE AND INQUIRY

CHAPTER 17: DIALOGIC INQUIRY AND ACTION RESEARCH

CHAPTER 18: CONCLUDING PERSPECTIVES ON ORGANIZATIONAL DEVELOPMENT

Thank you for picking up my book. Your support means a lot, and I hope you find the read both enjoyable and insightful. Beyond being an author, my work extends into research and consultancy within organizational behavior and leadership. I engage with a broad spectrum of clients, from individuals to larger teams and organizations, offering guidance in leadership development.

For a deeper dive into my professional background and consulting philosophy, several websites are available. There, you'll also find my contact details. I'm eager to hear your thoughts on the book or discuss potential collaboration in leadership coaching.

Discover more about my work and other publications related to leadership and organizational behavior at my personal website, https://thomaspatrickhuber.com.

Learn about my specific approach to leadership coaching and consulting at https://elevateus.ch, the official website of my company.

Lastly, in case you want to reach out to me directly please send me an email at thomaspatrick@mac.com.

I appreciate your support in purchasing this book and look forward to connecting with you.

Wishing you an enlightening journey,

Thomas P Huber, PhD, MS ECS

Dedication

To all the corporate organizational behavior and development consultants, managers, and leaders who tirelessly work to transform workplaces into thriving environments of collaboration, innovation, and growth.

To those who dedicate their careers to making organizations better, ensuring they are not only productive and efficient but also humane and fulfilling places to be. Your commitment to fostering positive change and enhancing the quality of work life is truly inspiring.

To the visionaries who strive to see beyond the status quo, always seeking new and improved ways of leading, managing, and developing people. Your relentless pursuit of excellence drives progress and sets new standards in organizational development.

To everyone who is passionate about learning, growing, and implementing better ways of being within organizations. Your quest for knowledge and continuous improvement fuels the evolution of our workplaces into spaces where everyone can succeed and feel valued.

This book is for you. Your efforts, insights, and unwavering commitment to positive change are the foundations upon which better organizations are built. Thank you for your dedication to creating workplaces where people can thrive and achieve their fullest potential.

Preface

Organizations face unprecedented challenges and opportunities. The rapid pace of technological advancement, shifting market demands, and the increasing importance of social and environmental responsibility require organizations to be more adaptive, innovative, and resilient than ever before. At the heart of navigating these complexities lies the field of Organizational Development (OD) and Change Management, a discipline dedicated to guiding organizations through the intricacies of transformation and growth.

This book, "The Change Imperative: Organizational Development for the 21st Century," is a comprehensive exploration of the theories, practices, and strategies that underpin successful organizational change. It is designed to serve as a valuable resource for consultants, managers, leaders, and anyone passionate about fostering positive change within their organizations. Whether you are a seasoned professional or a newcomer to the field, this book aims to equip you with the knowledge and tools needed to drive meaningful and sustainable transformation.

The journey of writing this book has been deeply influenced by the collaborative efforts and insights of many individuals. It is a reflection of the collective wisdom of countless practitioners who have dedicated their careers to understanding and improving organizational dynamics. Their experiences and contributions have enriched the content and have provided practical perspectives that bring the theoretical concepts to life.

In the chapters that follow, we delve into the foundational principles of OD, exploring the historical evolution of the field and the key theories that have shaped its development. We examine core concepts and approaches, from diagnostic models and change management strategies to team development and leadership enhancement. The book also addresses advanced topics such as improvisation in innovation, the importance of social networks, and the integration of mindfulness and stress reduction techniques in organizational practices. Furthermore, we extend our exploration to the global context, discussing the impact of globalization on labor markets and the increasing relevance of corporate social responsibility. We highlight the importance of diversity, inclusion, and social justice in creating equitable and thriving workplaces. Finally, we look ahead to emerging trends and innovative methods that promise to redefine the future of organizational development.

Writing this book has been a profound learning experience, offering new insights and deepening our understanding of the complex interplay between people, processes, and organizational structures. It is our hope that "The Change Imperative" will inspire you to embrace the principles of OD with enthusiasm and to apply them with creativity and rigor in your own organizational contexts.

Thank you for embarking on this journey with us. May this book serve as a guide and companion in your efforts to build organizations that are not only successful but also humane, inclusive, and sustainable.

Sincerely,

Thomas P Huber PhD MS ECS

Part I: Foundations of Organizational Development

Organizations must continuously adapt and evolve to remain competitive and relevant. This necessity for ongoing transformation is at the heart of Organizational Development (OD), a field dedicated to enhancing organizational effectiveness through planned change. Part I of this book, "Foundations of Organizational Development," provides a comprehensive overview of the fundamental principles and practices that form the bedrock of this dynamic discipline.

Chapter 1: Introduction to Organizational Development and Change

This chapter lays the groundwork for understanding OD by defining its scope and highlighting its importance in today's rapidly changing environment. We will trace the historical evolution of OD, examining key theories and milestones that have shaped its development. The role of change management will be explored, emphasizing its critical function in guiding organizations through transitions. Additionally, we will provide an overview of whole systems change, presenting a holistic approach to organizational transformation that addresses interconnected elements within the organization.

Chapter 2: Core Concepts and Approaches in Organizational Development

Building on the introduction, Chapter 2 delves into the core concepts and approaches that practitioners use to diagnose and address organizational challenges. We will discuss various diagnostic models and tools that help identify areas for improvement. The chapter will cover essential change management strategies and explore the dynamics of team development. Leadership development, a crucial aspect of OD, will be examined alongside strategies for shaping organizational culture. Finally, we will look at process consultation, a method for helping organizations improve their internal processes.

Chapter 3: Improvisation and Organizational Innovation

Innovation is vital for organizational growth and sustainability, and improvisation plays a key role in fostering a culture of creativity. This chapter will explore the role of creativity in organizations and how improvisation can enable agile responses to change. We will present case studies showcasing successful innovations that arose from improvisational practices. The chapter will also provide insights into building a culture of innovation, where creative problem-solving and flexibility are ingrained in the organizational ethos.

Chapter 4: Organizational Strategy and Learning

Effective organizations align their strategies with continuous learning and adaptation. Chapter 4 examines various theories and models of organizational learning, including the Resource-Based View (RBV) and Knowledge-Based View (KBV). We will explore the Dynamic Capabilities Framework, which emphasizes the ability to integrate, build, and reconfigure internal and external competencies. The chapter will also discuss how to align strategy with organizational learning, ensuring that learning initiatives support strategic objectives. The importance of continuous improvement and adaptation will be highlighted as essential elements of a resilient organization.

Chapter 5: Social Network Analysis

Understanding the informal networks within an organization is crucial for fostering communication, innovation, and effective leadership. This chapter introduces Social Network Analysis (SNA) as a tool for visualizing and analyzing social relationships. We will explore the importance of social networks in organizations and the tools and methods used in SNA. Practical applications of SNA in enhancing communication, driving innovation, and identifying leadership dynamics will be discussed, providing a comprehensive view of how informal networks influence organizational performance.

By the end of Part I, readers will have a solid foundation in the principles and practices of Organizational Development. This knowledge will serve as a crucial stepping stone for exploring more advanced concepts and strategies in subsequent parts of the book. The insights gained here will empower practitioners to implement effective OD initiatives that drive sustainable growth and transformation in their organizations.

Chapter 1: Introduction to Organizational Development and Change

The ability of an organization to adapt, evolve, and thrive amidst change is not merely an advantage—it is a necessity. Organizational Development (OD) is the field dedicated to facilitating this adaptability through strategic, systematic, and intentional interventions. This chapter serves as an introduction to the fundamental concepts of OD and change management, setting the stage for deeper exploration in subsequent chapters.

Organizational Development is defined as a planned, organization-wide effort to increase an organization's effectiveness and viability. Rooted in the behavioral sciences, OD involves the application of various strategies and methodologies to enhance organizational health, improve performance, and facilitate growth. The importance of OD lies in its holistic approach to managing change, fostering a culture of continuous improvement, and aligning the organization's structures, processes, and people with its strategic goals. In an era where change is constant, the principles of OD help organizations remain resilient and competitive.

The field of Organizational Development has evolved significantly since its inception in the mid-20th century. Its roots can be traced back to the human relations movement and the work of early pioneers like Kurt Lewin, who introduced foundational concepts such as action research and the unfreeze-change-refreeze model of change. Over the decades, OD has integrated various theories from psychology, sociology, and management science. Key theories that have shaped the field include systems theory, which views organizations as complex and interrelated systems, and the resource-based view, which emphasizes the strategic importance of developing unique internal capabilities.

Change management is a critical component of Organizational Development, focusing specifically on the processes and strategies used to manage the people side of change. Effective change management ensures that transitions are smooth and that the desired outcomes of change initiatives are achieved. It involves preparing, supporting, and helping individuals, teams, and organizations to adopt new ways of working. Change management addresses potential resistance to change, engages stakeholders, and aligns organizational goals with change initiatives to ensure successful implementation.

Whole systems change represents a holistic approach to organizational transformation. Rather than focusing on individual parts in isolation, this approach considers the organization as an interconnected system. Whole systems change aims to create comprehensive and sustainable transformations by addressing interdependencies within the organization. This involves mapping and understanding the organization's systems, identifying leverage points for change, and implementing strategies that impact the entire system. By adopting a whole systems perspective, organizations can drive significant improvements that are integrated and aligned with their overall mission and objectives.

As we embark on this journey through the intricacies of Organizational Development and change management, this chapter lays the foundation by introducing the key concepts and historical context that underpin the field. Understanding the definition, importance, and evolution of OD, along with the critical role of change management and the principles of whole systems change, provides a comprehensive starting point. These foundational elements will be elaborated upon and applied in practical contexts throughout the rest of this book, equipping you with the knowledge and tools necessary to drive effective and sustainable change in your organization.

Organizational Development (OD) is a systematic and planned effort aimed at improving an organization's effectiveness, efficiency, and health. Rooted in the behavioral sciences, OD involves the application of various methodologies to foster positive change in organizational structures, processes, and culture. It encompasses a wide range of activities, including strategic planning, leadership development, team building, and process improvement. The goal of OD is to enhance the organization's capacity to handle internal and external challenges, promoting sustained growth and development.

The importance of OD cannot be overstated, especially in today's fast-paced and competitive business environment. OD equips organizations with the tools and strategies needed to respond effectively to changes in the external environment, such as market shifts, technological advancements, and regulatory changes. Through systematic interventions, OD helps in optimizing processes, improving efficiency, and increasing productivity, leading to better overall organizational performance. OD initiatives often focus on improving workplace culture, communication, and team dynamics, which can lead to higher levels of employee engagement and job satisfaction. Additionally, OD ensures that the organization's goals, processes, and resources are aligned with its strategic vision, helping achieve long-term objectives and sustaining competitive advantage. By fostering a culture of continuous improvement and learning, OD encourages innovation and creativity, enabling organizations to become better at problem-solving and adapting new ideas and technologies.

Change management is a structured approach to transitioning individuals, teams, and organizations from a current state to a desired future state. It involves the application of tools, processes, and techniques to manage the people side of change, ensuring that change initiatives are implemented smoothly and achieve their intended outcomes. Change management addresses the human aspects of change, including managing resistance, engaging stakeholders, and fostering a culture that embraces change.

The importance of change management lies in its ability to ensure successful implementation of change initiatives. Change often meets with resistance from employees who are accustomed to existing ways of working. Change management helps in addressing and reducing this resistance through communication, involvement, and support. Effective change management ensures that new processes, technologies, or strategies are adopted more quickly and effectively, leading to faster realization of benefits. By involving employees in the change process and addressing their concerns, change management helps in maintaining morale and engagement during transitions. It ensures that change initiatives are aligned with the organization's strategic goals, enhancing the likelihood of achieving desired outcomes. Change management focuses not only on implementing change but also on sustaining it. This involves embedding new behaviors and practices into the organizational culture to ensure long-term success.

Organizational Development and Change Management are interrelated disciplines that play a critical role in helping organizations navigate and thrive amidst change. OD provides the framework for systematic improvement and capacity building, while change management focuses on the human aspects of transitioning to new ways of working. Together, they enable organizations to adapt, grow, and achieve sustained success in an ever-changing business landscape.

The field of Organizational Development (OD) has evolved significantly since its inception in the mid-20th century. Its roots can be traced back to the human relations movement and the work of early pioneers like Kurt Lewin, who introduced foundational concepts such as action research and the unfreeze-change-refreeze model of change. Over the decades, OD has integrated various theories from psychology, sociology, and management science, shaping its development into a comprehensive approach to organizational improvement.

Kurt Lewin's contributions were pivotal, particularly his work on group dynamics and change processes. His action research model emphasized a collaborative approach to problem-solving, where researchers and participants work together to diagnose issues and implement solutions. The unfreeze-change-refreeze model provided a framework for understanding how to manage change effectively by preparing an organization for change, implementing the change, and solidifying the new behaviors and processes.

The Tavistock Institute in the UK also played a significant role in the early development of OD, particularly through its studies on group behavior and organizational dynamics. The socio-technical systems theory emerged from this work, highlighting the interdependence between social and technical systems in organizations. This theory emphasized the
importance of balancing these systems to optimize organizational performance and employee satisfaction.

Douglas McGregor's Theory X and Theory Y introduced in the 1960s, provided a new perspective on management styles and employee motivation. Theory X assumes that employees are inherently lazy and require strict supervision, while Theory Y posits that employees are self-motivated and seek responsibility. McGregor's work underscored the importance of managerial assumptions in shaping organizational culture and employee behavior, promoting a more humanistic approach to management that aligns with OD principles.

Chris Argyris and Donald Schön contributed significantly to OD with their concepts of single-loop and double-loop learning. Single-loop learning involves making corrections without altering underlying norms, while double-loop learning requires questioning and modifying these norms. This deeper level of learning enables organizations to adapt more profoundly to changing environments and is fundamental to continuous improvement.

In the 1980s and 1990s, Peter Senge's work on learning organizations further advanced OD theory. His book "The Fifth Discipline" introduced the idea that organizations should be seen as complex systems where individuals continually expand their capacity to create desired results. Senge's five disciplines—systems thinking, personal mastery, mental models, shared vision, and team learning—provided a framework for fostering an organizational culture of continuous learning and adaptation.

The Resource-Based View (RBV) and the Knowledge-Based View (KBV) of the firm emerged as influential theories in the late 20th century. RBV focuses on developing unique internal resources and capabilities that provide competitive advantage, while KBV emphasizes the strategic importance of knowledge creation, sharing, and utilization within the organization. These theories highlight the role of internal capabilities and knowledge in achieving and sustaining competitive advantage.

The Dynamic Capabilities Framework, building on RBV and KBV, addresses the need for organizations to continuously integrate, build, and reconfigure internal and external competencies to respond to rapidly changing environments. This framework underscores the importance of learning, innovation, and agility in maintaining organizational competitiveness.

Over the years, OD has evolved from focusing primarily on individual and group behavior to encompassing broader organizational systems and strategic alignment. It has integrated insights from various disciplines, making it a multifaceted approach to enhancing organizational effectiveness. By understanding and applying these key theories, organizations can navigate complex changes and achieve sustained growth and development.

Change management is essential for ensuring that organizational transitions are smooth and effective. It focuses on the people side of change, addressing how individuals, teams, and the entire organization adapt to new processes, technologies, and strategies. The primary role of change management is to prepare, support, and guide these transitions to achieve successful outcomes. Effective change management involves clear and consistent communication to explain the need for change and its benefits, reducing uncertainty and building trust. It engages stakeholders at all levels, ensuring their involvement and buy-in, which is crucial for minimizing resistance and fostering a sense of ownership.

One of the critical aspects of change management is identifying and addressing potential resistance. This involves understanding the concerns and fears of employees and providing the necessary support to help them through the transition. This support can take various forms, including training programs to develop new skills, resources to ease the transition, and counseling to address emotional and psychological impacts.

Change management also ensures alignment between the change initiative and the organization's strategic goals. This alignment is crucial for maintaining focus and coherence throughout the transition process. By linking change efforts to strategic objectives, change management helps ensure that the changes contribute to the organization's long-term success and competitiveness.

Monitoring and evaluation are integral components of effective change management. These processes involve assessing the progress of the change initiative, identifying any issues or obstacles, and making necessary adjustments to stay on track. Continuous feedback mechanisms allow for real-time improvements and ensure that the change initiative remains relevant and effective.

Sustaining change is another vital role of change management. This involves embedding new behaviors, processes, and practices into the organizational culture to ensure that the change is lasting. It requires ongoing reinforcement through policies, incentives, and regular assessments to prevent regression to old ways of working.

Change management is a structured approach to navigating organizational transitions. It emphasizes clear communication, stakeholder engagement, support for individuals, strategic alignment, continuous monitoring, and sustaining change. By focusing on these areas, change management helps organizations adapt successfully to new challenges and opportunities, ensuring long-term effectiveness and resilience.

Whole systems change is a holistic approach to organizational transformation that considers the organization as an interconnected and interdependent entity. Instead of focusing on individual components in isolation, this approach examines how different parts of the organization interact and influence each other. The goal of whole systems change is to create comprehensive and sustainable transformations by addressing these interdependencies and leveraging the collective potential of the organization.

At the heart of whole systems change is systems thinking, which involves understanding the organization as a complex system with various elements that are dynamically connected. This perspective helps identify patterns, relationships, and feedback loops that influence organizational behavior and outcomes. By recognizing these connections, leaders can develop strategies that target the root causes of issues rather than just addressing symptoms.

Mapping and understanding organizational systems are crucial steps in whole systems change. This process involves creating visual representations of the organization's structures, processes, and relationships, which can reveal critical points of leverage. Identifying these leverage points allows for targeted interventions that can have a significant impact on the entire system. This strategic approach ensures that changes are not only effective but also aligned with the organization's overall goals and values.

Implementing whole systems change requires a collaborative effort that engages stakeholders from across the organization. Involving employees, managers, and other key stakeholders in the change process helps build a shared understanding and commitment to the desired outcomes. This inclusive approach fosters a sense of ownership and accountability, which is essential for the success and sustainability of the change initiative.

Case studies of whole systems change highlight the practical application and benefits of this approach. These examples demonstrate how organizations have successfully navigated complex transformations by addressing multiple aspects of their systems simultaneously. They illustrate the importance of a coordinated and integrated strategy that considers the interplay between various elements of the organization.

Whole systems change is a holistic approach that focuses on the interconnected nature of organizational components. It leverages systems thinking to identify and address root causes, involves mapping and understanding organizational systems, and engages stakeholders in a collaborative effort. This comprehensive method aims to create sustainable and aligned transformations that enhance the overall effectiveness and resilience of the organization.

We have laid the groundwork for understanding Organizational Development (OD) and Change Management, two crucial disciplines for navigating the complexities of modern business environments. We began by defining OD, emphasizing its role in enhancing organizational effectiveness, efficiency, and health through systematic and planned interventions. We highlighted the importance of OD in fostering adaptability, improving performance, engaging employees, and driving innovation and strategic alignment.

We then traced the historical evolution of OD, exploring key theories and contributions from pioneers like Kurt Lewin, Douglas McGregor, Chris Argyris, and Peter Senge. These foundational theories—ranging from action research and socio-technical systems to single-loop and double-loop learning and the concept of learning organizations—provide a rich framework for understanding how organizations can continuously learn and improve.

The role of change management was also discussed, focusing on its critical function in managing the human aspects of organizational transitions. Effective change management involves clear communication, stakeholder engagement, resistance management, alignment with strategic goals, continuous monitoring, and sustaining change. These elements ensure that organizational changes are implemented smoothly and achieve their intended outcomes.

We introduced the concept of whole systems change, a holistic approach that views the organization as an interconnected system. Systems thinking, mapping organizational systems, identifying leverage points, and engaging stakeholders in collaborative efforts are key components of this approach. Whole systems change aims to create comprehensive and sustainable transformations by addressing interdependencies within the organization.

It is essential to recognize that the journey of Organizational Development and Change Management is one of continuous learning and adaptation. The principles and practices we have discussed provide a foundation for navigating the complexities of change, but their application requires creativity, resilience, and a commitment to fostering a culture of improvement.

Inspiration lies in the potential of OD and change management to transform organizations into thriving entities that not only achieve their goals but also create environments where people can flourish. By embracing these disciplines, you are embarking on a path that can lead to significant and lasting positive change. As you move forward, remember that every challenge is an opportunity for growth, and every change initiative is a step toward building a more adaptive, innovative, and resilient organization.

This book will continue to build on these foundational concepts, offering deeper insights and practical strategies to help you drive effective and sustainable change. Together, we will explore the advanced methodologies, global perspectives, and innovative approaches that will equip you to lead your organization confidently into the future.

Chapter 2: Core Concepts and Approaches in Organizational Development

In Chapter 2, we dig deeper into the essential concepts and methodologies that form the backbone of Organizational Development (OD). This chapter provides a comprehensive exploration of the core approaches that practitioners use to diagnose and address organizational challenges, implement change, and foster a thriving organizational culture. Understanding these fundamental elements is crucial for anyone involved in guiding organizations through the complexities of transformation and growth.

Diagnostic models and tools are vital in identifying areas for improvement within an organization. These models and tools offer systematic methods for analyzing organizational structures, processes, and behaviors, providing a clear picture of current performance and pinpointing underlying issues. Through effective diagnosis, organizations can develop targeted interventions that address specific problems and capitalize on opportunities for enhancement.

Change management strategies are integral to ensuring that organizational changes are implemented smoothly and effectively. These strategies encompass a variety of techniques designed to manage the human side of change, including communication plans, stakeholder engagement, training programs, and support systems. By employing robust change management strategies, organizations can minimize resistance, foster buy-in, and ensure that changes are sustainable over the long term.

Team development and dynamics focus on enhancing the performance and cohesion of work groups within the organization.

Effective team development involves understanding the stages of team formation, promoting effective communication, and leveraging the diverse strengths of team members. This section explores how to build high-performing teams that are capable of collaborating effectively and achieving collective goals.

Leadership development is a critical component of OD, as effective leadership is essential for driving change and guiding organizations toward their strategic objectives. This part of the chapter examines the skills and behaviors that characterize strong leaders and offers strategies for developing these attributes within the organization. Leadership development initiatives can include formal training programs, mentorship, and experiential learning opportunities designed to cultivate leaders who can inspire and motivate their teams.

Shaping organizational culture involves influencing the values, beliefs, and behaviors that define the way work is performed within the organization. A strong, positive culture can enhance employee engagement, improve performance, and attract top talent. This section discusses methods for assessing and shaping organizational culture, ensuring that it aligns with the organization's strategic goals and supports a healthy, productive work environment.

Process consultation is a collaborative approach to helping organizations improve their internal processes. This method involves working closely with organizational members to diagnose issues, design interventions, and implement changes that enhance efficiency and effectiveness. Process consultation emphasizes the importance of involving employees in the change process, fostering a sense of ownership and commitment to continuous improvement.

As we explore these core concepts and approaches in Organizational Development, this chapter aims to equip you with the knowledge and tools necessary to diagnose issues, implement effective change strategies, and foster a positive and productive organizational environment. Each section provides practical insights and real-world examples to illustrate how these concepts can be applied to drive meaningful and sustainable improvements. By mastering these foundational elements, you will be well-prepared to navigate the complexities of organizational development and lead your organization to greater success.

Diagnostic models and tools are essential instruments in Organizational Development (OD), providing a structured approach to understanding and addressing organizational issues. These models and tools help practitioners systematically analyze various aspects of the organization, identify problems, and develop targeted interventions to enhance performance and effectiveness.

One widely used diagnostic model is the McKinsey 7-S Framework. This model examines seven interrelated elements of an organization: strategy, structure, systems, shared values, style, staff, and skills. By assessing how these elements align and interact, practitioners can identify areas of misalignment and opportunities for improvement. The 7-S Framework helps ensure that all parts of the organization are working cohesively towards common goals.

Another important tool is SWOT analysis, which stands for strengths, weaknesses, opportunities, and threats. This analysis provides a comprehensive overview of internal and external factors that can impact organizational performance. By identifying strengths and weaknesses within the organization, along with external opportunities and threats, leaders can develop strategies that leverage strengths, mitigate weaknesses, capitalize on opportunities, and defend against threats. SWOT analysis is particularly useful for strategic planning and decision-making.

The Burke-Litwin Model of Organizational Performance and Change is another valuable diagnostic tool. This model explores the causal relationships between various organizational variables, such as external environment, leadership, mission and strategy, culture, structure, management practices, systems, work climate, task requirements, motivation, and individual and organizational performance. By understanding these relationships, practitioners can pinpoint the root causes of performance issues and design interventions that address these underlying factors.

Organizational Culture Assessment Instrument (OCAI) is used to evaluate an organization's culture. Developed by Cameron and Quinn, this tool categorizes organizational culture into four types: clan, adhocracy, market, and hierarchy. By assessing the current and preferred culture profiles, organizations can identify cultural gaps and develop strategies to move towards a more desired cultural state. This tool is particularly useful for culture change initiatives.

Six Sigma and Lean methodologies offer diagnostic tools focused on process improvement and efficiency. Six Sigma uses statistical analysis to identify and reduce variability in processes, aiming for near-perfect quality. Lean methodology focuses on eliminating waste and improving workflow efficiency. Both methodologies involve a range of diagnostic tools, such as process mapping, root cause analysis, and value stream mapping, which help organizations streamline operations and enhance productivity.

Employee surveys and feedback tools are also crucial for diagnosing organizational health. These tools gather insights directly from employees about their experiences, satisfaction, engagement, and perceptions of the workplace. By analyzing this feedback, organizations can identify areas where employees feel supported and areas needing improvement. Regular use of employee surveys helps track progress over time and ensures that interventions are responsive to employee needs.

Diagnostic models and tools provide a systematic approach to understanding and addressing organizational issues. By using frameworks like the McKinsey 7-S, SWOT analysis, Burke-Litwin Model, OCAI, Six Sigma, Lean methodologies, and employee surveys, practitioners can gain a comprehensive understanding of organizational dynamics and develop targeted interventions to enhance performance, culture, and overall effectiveness. These tools are fundamental to the practice of

Organizational Development, enabling leaders to make informed decisions and drive sustainable improvements.

Change management strategies are essential for guiding organizations through transitions, ensuring that changes are effectively implemented and sustained. These strategies focus on the human side of change, addressing how individuals and groups adapt to new processes, technologies, and ways of working. A successful change management strategy begins with clear and consistent communication. This involves articulating the vision for change, explaining the reasons behind it, and outlining the benefits. Transparent communication helps reduce uncertainty and build trust among employees, making them more likely to support the change.

Engaging stakeholders is another critical component. Involving employees, managers, and other key stakeholders in the change process fosters a sense of ownership and commitment. This can be achieved through workshops, focus groups, and regular updates, ensuring that everyone has a voice and understands their role in the transition. Providing support and training is essential for equipping employees with the skills and knowledge they need to adapt to new systems or processes. This includes offering formal training sessions, creating resource materials, and providing access to support networks where employees can ask questions and share experiences.

Managing resistance is a common challenge in change initiatives. Identifying potential sources of resistance early on allows for proactive measures to address concerns and mitigate negative impacts. This might involve one-on-one meetings with resistant individuals, addressing their specific concerns, and demonstrating how the change benefits them personally. Continuous monitoring and feedback mechanisms are crucial for tracking progress and identifying areas where adjustments are needed. Regularly soliciting feedback from employees helps to ensure that the change initiative remains on track and responsive to any emerging issues.

Aligning the change initiative with the organization's strategic goals is vital for maintaining focus and coherence. This alignment ensures that all efforts are directed towards achieving the desired outcomes and that the change supports the organization's long-term vision. Leadership plays a pivotal role in change management. Effective leaders model the behaviors they wish to see in others, demonstrate commitment to the change, and provide ongoing support and encouragement. Leadership involvement is key to maintaining momentum and inspiring confidence throughout the organization.

Embedding change into the organizational culture ensures that new practices and behaviors become the norm. This involves reinforcing the change through policies, incentives, and regular assessments. Celebrating milestones and recognizing achievements along the way helps to sustain motivation and reinforce the value of the change. By implementing these strategies, organizations can navigate the complexities of change, minimize disruptions, and achieve lasting benefits. Effective change management not only facilitates successful transitions but also builds a more resilient and adaptable organization, capable of thriving in a constantly evolving business environment.

Team development and dynamics are critical components of organizational success, focusing on enhancing the performance and cohesion of work groups. Effective team development begins with establishing clear goals and roles. It is essential for every team member to understand the team's objectives and how their individual contributions align with these goals. This clarity ensures that efforts are coordinated and that everyone is working towards a common purpose.

Fostering open communication within the team is crucial. Creating an environment where team members feel safe to express their thoughts, ideas, and concerns without fear of judgment promotes transparency and trust. Regular meetings, whether in-person or virtual, help keep team members aligned and informed, facilitating effective collaboration and problem-solving.

Building trust and respect among team members is fundamental for a cohesive team dynamic. Trust-building activities and opportunities for team members to share and collaborate can deepen relationships and enhance mutual respect. Valuing diverse perspectives and acknowledging each contribution reinforces a culture of respect and inclusivity, encouraging everyone to participate fully.

Leveraging team strengths involves understanding the unique skills and abilities of each team member. By identifying individual strengths and weaknesses through assessments or workshops, tasks and responsibilities can be assigned in a way that plays to each member's strengths. This approach not only enhances team efficiency but also boosts job satisfaction, as team members are more likely to be engaged when they are working in areas where they excel.

Promoting team collaboration is essential for achieving high performance. Encouraging collaborative problem-solving allows the team to draw on a wide range of perspectives and ideas, leading to more innovative and effective solutions. Utilizing collaboration tools and platforms can facilitate seamless communication and coordination, particularly for remote or distributed teams.

Recognizing and rewarding team performance is a key motivator. Regularly acknowledging individual and team achievements boosts morale and motivation. Implementing reward systems that align with team goals fosters a sense of accomplishment and reinforces the desired behaviors and outcomes.

Monitoring and adjusting team dynamics is an ongoing process. Regular assessments of team health, such as surveys or feedback tools, help gauge morale, dynamics, and effectiveness. Being open to restructuring teams, revising roles, or addressing conflicts as needed ensures that the team remains effective and aligned with organizational goals.

Facilitating team bonding through organized activities outside of regular work tasks can help break down barriers and improve relationships among team members. Celebrating successes together reinforces a sense of unity and shared purpose, contributing to a positive and collaborative team environment.

Effective team development and dynamics are essential for organizational success. By fostering open communication, building trust and respect, leveraging team strengths, promoting collaboration, recognizing achievements, and continuously monitoring and adjusting team dynamics, organizations can build high-performing teams capable of achieving collective goals and driving success.

Leadership development is a crucial aspect of organizational growth and success, focusing on enhancing the skills, behaviors, and capabilities of current and potential leaders within the organization. Effective leadership development begins with identifying the key competencies and attributes that define strong leaders. These may include strategic thinking, emotional intelligence, effective communication, and the ability to inspire and motivate others.

Organizations must provide opportunities for leaders to develop these competencies through formal training programs. These programs can include workshops, seminars, and courses that cover essential leadership topics such as decision-making, conflict resolution, and change management. Beyond formal education, experiential learning opportunities, such as challenging assignments, cross-functional projects, and rotational roles, allow leaders to apply their skills in real-world scenarios, fostering practical experience and growth.

Mentorship and coaching are also vital components of leadership development. Pairing emerging leaders with experienced mentors provides guidance, support, and valuable insights. Mentors can help mentees navigate complex organizational dynamics, set career goals, and develop strategies for achieving them. Coaching, on the other hand, offers personalized feedback and helps leaders refine their skills, address specific challenges, and enhance their overall effectiveness.

Leadership development should also focus on self-awareness and personal growth. Tools such as 360-degree feedback, personality assessments, and reflective exercises can help leaders gain insights into their strengths and areas for improvement. This self-awareness is crucial for personal development and for understanding how to better lead and support their teams.

Creating a culture of continuous learning and development is essential for sustaining leadership growth. Organizations should encourage leaders to seek out new knowledge, stay updated with industry trends, and continually refine their skills. This can be facilitated through access to online learning platforms, attendance at industry conferences, and participation in professional networks.

Recognizing and rewarding leadership development efforts reinforces the importance of ongoing growth and sets a positive example for others in the organization. Acknowledging leaders who demonstrate significant improvement and impact can motivate them and others to invest in their development.

Leadership development is not a one-time initiative but a continuous process that evolves with the changing needs of the organization and the external environment. By providing comprehensive training, fostering mentorship and coaching relationships, encouraging self-awareness, and promoting a culture of continuous learning, organizations can cultivate strong leaders who are well-equipped to drive success and inspire their teams. Effective leadership development ensures that the organization has a pipeline of capable leaders ready to meet future challenges and opportunities.

Shaping organizational culture involves influencing the values, beliefs, and behaviors that define how work is performed within an organization. A strong, positive culture can enhance employee engagement, improve performance, and attract top talent. The process begins with understanding the current culture through assessments and feedback from employees. This can include surveys, focus groups, and interviews to gather insights into the existing values, norms, and behaviors that characterize the organization.

Leadership plays a pivotal role in shaping and modeling the desired culture. Leaders must embody the values and behaviors they wish to see in their teams. By setting an example through their actions, they can influence the organizational climate and encourage others to follow suit. Consistent and transparent communication from leaders about the importance of cultural values and the behaviors that support them reinforces the desired culture.

Creating and promoting a shared vision is crucial for aligning employees with the organizational culture. This vision should articulate the core values and principles that guide the organization's actions and decisions. When employees understand and buy into this vision, it fosters a sense of purpose and direction, aligning their efforts with the organization's goals.

Recognizing and rewarding behaviors that align with the desired culture helps reinforce these behaviors and embed them into the organizational fabric. This can involve formal recognition programs, rewards, and incentives that celebrate individuals and teams who exemplify the organization's values. Such recognition not only motivates employees but also signals to the entire organization what is valued and expected.

Incorporating cultural values into the organization's policies, procedures, and practices ensures that the culture is consistently applied and reinforced. This might include integrating cultural values into hiring and onboarding processes, performance management systems, and training programs. By embedding these values into the daily operations of the organization, they become a natural part of how work is conducted.

Encouraging open and ongoing dialogue about the culture allows for continuous feedback and improvement. Employees should feel comfortable discussing cultural issues and suggesting ways to enhance the organizational environment. This openness fosters a sense of ownership and accountability among employees, contributing to a dynamic and evolving culture.

Shaping organizational culture is an ongoing process that requires commitment and active participation from all levels of the organization. It involves understanding the current culture, modeling desired behaviors, creating a shared vision, recognizing and rewarding aligned behaviors, embedding values into policies and practices, and encouraging open dialogue. By focusing on these elements, organizations can cultivate a positive, cohesive culture that supports their strategic objectives and enhances overall performance.

Process consultation is a collaborative approach to organizational development that focuses on improving internal processes and enhancing overall effectiveness. This method involves a close partnership between the consultant and the organization, where the consultant helps diagnose issues, design interventions, and implement changes that foster better performance and efficiency. The core of process consultation lies in engaging organizational members in identifying and solving their own problems, promoting a sense of ownership and accountability.

The process begins with entry and contracting, where the consultant and the organization establish a clear agreement on the objectives, scope, and expectations of the consultation. This stage sets the foundation for a successful collaboration by ensuring mutual understanding and commitment to the process.

Diagnosis and data collection are crucial steps in process consultation. The consultant works with organizational members to gather information about the current processes, workflows, and interactions. This can involve interviews, surveys, observations, and reviewing existing documentation. The goal is to gain a comprehensive understanding of the organization's functioning and identify areas that need improvement.

Feedback and joint problem-solving are integral to process consultation. The consultant provides feedback to the organization based on the diagnostic data, highlighting key findings and areas for improvement. Together, the consultant and organizational members engage in collaborative discussions to develop action plans that address the identified issues. This participatory approach ensures that solutions are practical, relevant, and tailored to the organization's specific needs.

Implementation of the agreed-upon interventions follows, with the consultant providing support and guidance throughout the process. This may involve training sessions, workshops, or hands-on assistance to help employees adopt new practices and behaviors. The consultant's role is to facilitate change rather than dictate solutions, empowering organizational members to take charge of the improvement efforts.

Continuous evaluation and follow-up are essential components of process consultation. Regular assessments are conducted to monitor progress, measure the impact of the interventions, and identify any emerging issues. This iterative process allows for adjustments and refinements to ensure that the changes are effective and sustainable.

Process consultation emphasizes building the organization's capacity for self-diagnosis and continuous improvement. By involving employees in the diagnostic and problem-solving processes, it enhances their skills and confidence in managing future challenges. This approach not only addresses immediate issues but also fosters a culture of learning and adaptability within the organization.

Process consultation is a collaborative and participatory approach to organizational development that focuses on improving internal processes through diagnosis, feedback, joint problem-solving, implementation, and continuous evaluation. By engaging organizational members in these activities, it promotes a sense of ownership, enhances capabilities, and fosters a culture of continuous improvement, ultimately leading to better organizational performance and effectiveness.

Chapter 2 of this book has explored the core concepts and approaches in Organizational Development (OD), providing a comprehensive understanding of the tools and strategies essential for fostering effective organizational change. We have explored diagnostic models and tools, which offer a structured approach to analyzing and understanding organizational issues. These models, such as the McKinsey 7-S Framework, SWOT analysis, Burke-Litwin Model, Organizational Culture Assessment Instrument (OCAI), Six Sigma, and Lean methodologies, enable practitioners to identify areas for improvement and develop targeted interventions.

We discussed change management strategies that ensure smooth and effective transitions within organizations. Emphasizing communication, stakeholder engagement, support and training, managing resistance, continuous monitoring, and embedding change into the organizational culture, these strategies address the human aspects of change to ensure sustainable outcomes.

Team development and dynamics were also covered, highlighting the importance of clear goals, open communication, trust, leveraging strengths, promoting collaboration, recognizing achievements, and continuously monitoring team health. Effective team development fosters high-performing teams that can drive organizational success.

Leadership development was examined, focusing on enhancing the skills, behaviors, and capabilities of current and potential leaders. Through formal training, experiential learning, mentorship, coaching, self-awareness tools, and continuous learning, organizations can cultivate leaders who are equipped to inspire and guide their teams.

Shaping organizational culture involves influencing values, beliefs, and behaviors to create a cohesive and productive work environment. By understanding the current culture, modeling desired behaviors, creating a shared vision, recognizing aligned behaviors, embedding values into policies, and encouraging open dialogue, organizations can build a positive culture that supports strategic goals.

Process consultation, a collaborative approach to improving internal processes, was also explored. This method emphasizes engagement, diagnosis, feedback, joint problem-solving, implementation, and continuous evaluation, empowering organizational members to take ownership of improvement efforts and fostering a culture of learning and adaptability.

The core concepts and approaches discussed in this chapter provide the foundation for effective Organizational Development. By applying these tools and strategies, practitioners can diagnose issues, implement changes, and foster a positive organizational environment that supports continuous improvement and sustainable success. As we move forward in this book, we will build on these foundational elements, exploring advanced methodologies and innovative approaches to further enhance your ability to drive meaningful change within your organization. Through commitment, collaboration, and a focus on continuous learning, you can lead your organization towards a thriving future.

Chapter 3: Improvisation and Organizational Innovation

The ability to innovate and adapt quickly is crucial for organizational success. This chapter explores the role of improvisation and creativity in fostering organizational innovation. We will examine how these elements enable organizations to respond agilely to change, drive continuous improvement, and maintain a competitive edge. By understanding and harnessing the power of creativity and improvisation, organizations can build a culture that supports and sustains innovation.

Creativity serves as the foundation for innovation within organizations. It involves generating new and valuable ideas that can solve existing problems, improve processes, or create entirely new products and services. Creative thinking encourages employees to look beyond conventional solutions and explore novel approaches. This mindset not only enhances problem-solving capabilities but also drives the development of unique competitive advantages. Encouraging creativity at all levels of the organization fosters an environment where innovation can thrive.

Improvisation, often associated with artistic endeavors such as jazz music and theater, has significant applications in the business world. It involves the spontaneous and flexible response to unexpected challenges and opportunities. Unlike traditional approaches that rely heavily on extensive planning and predictability, improvisation emphasizes agility, adaptability, and quick decision-making based on the current situation. This ability to pivot and adapt in real-time is invaluable in a rapidly changing business landscape, where unforeseen circumstances can arise at any moment.

Through various case studies, we will illustrate how organizations have successfully leveraged improvisation to drive innovation. These examples will demonstrate how embracing improvisational techniques can lead to breakthrough solutions and significant competitive advantages. By studying these cases, we can extract valuable lessons and best practices that can be applied to other organizational contexts.

Building a culture of innovation requires more than just encouraging creativity and improvisation. It involves creating an environment where risk-taking is supported, failure is seen as a learning opportunity, and continuous improvement is ingrained in the organizational DNA. Leaders play a crucial role in fostering this culture by modeling innovative behaviors, providing resources and support for creative initiatives, and recognizing and rewarding innovative efforts. By embedding these principles into the organizational culture, companies can sustain innovation and remain agile in the face of change.

This chapter aims to provide a comprehensive understanding of how improvisation and creativity contribute to organizational innovation. We will explore practical strategies for fostering these elements within your organization and examine real-world examples of their successful application. By embracing improvisation and building a culture of innovation, you can enhance your organization's ability to adapt, compete, and thrive in a dynamic business environment.

Creativity is the lifeblood of innovation within organizations, serving as the foundation upon which new ideas and solutions are built. It involves the ability to think beyond conventional boundaries, to envision possibilities that others may not see, and to develop novel approaches to existing challenges. In a business context, creativity is not limited to artistic endeavors but encompasses all aspects of organizational life, from product development and marketing to process improvement and strategic planning.

Encouraging creativity within an organization starts with fostering an environment that supports experimentation and risk-taking. This means creating a culture where employees feel safe to express their ideas without fear of criticism or failure. When failure is viewed as a learning opportunity rather than a setback, employees are more likely to take bold steps and propose innovative solutions. Leaders play a crucial role in this by modeling creative behaviors, providing resources and time for creative activities, and recognizing and rewarding creative efforts.

Creativity drives competitive advantage by enabling organizations to differentiate themselves in the marketplace. Innovative products, services, and processes can set a company apart from its competitors, attracting customers and driving growth. Moreover, creative problem-solving can lead to more efficient and effective operations, reducing costs and increasing productivity. By continuously seeking creative solutions, organizations can stay ahead of industry trends and adapt more quickly to changing market conditions.

Interdisciplinary collaboration is a powerful driver of creativity. When people from diverse backgrounds and areas of expertise come together, they bring different perspectives and ideas that can spark innovative thinking. Encouraging cross-functional teams and fostering a collaborative work environment can lead to breakthroughs that might not emerge within siloed departments. This approach not only enhances creativity but also builds a more cohesive and integrated organization.

Technology also plays a significant role in fostering creativity within organizations. Tools and platforms that facilitate idea generation, collaboration, and prototyping can help employees bring their creative ideas to life more quickly and effectively. Technology can also provide access to a wealth of information and inspiration, expanding the creative potential of individuals and teams.

Creativity is essential for long-term sustainability and growth. Organizations that prioritize and nurture creativity are better equipped to navigate the uncertainties and complexities of the modern business landscape. They are more resilient, adaptable, and capable of seizing new opportunities as they arise. By embedding creativity into the organizational culture, companies can ensure that innovation remains a constant driving force, leading to sustained success and a competitive edge.

Improvisation in an organizational context involves the ability to spontaneously and effectively respond to unexpected challenges and opportunities. Unlike traditional approaches that rely on extensive planning and predictability, improvisation emphasizes flexibility, adaptability, and quick decision-making based on the current situation. This capacity to pivot and adjust in real-time is invaluable in a rapidly changing business environment where unforeseen circumstances can arise at any moment.

An agile response to change is crucial for maintaining competitiveness and relevance. Organizations that can quickly adapt to shifts in the market, technological advancements, and evolving consumer expectations are better positioned to capitalize on new opportunities and mitigate risks. Improvisation enables teams to devise creative solutions on the fly, leveraging their collective knowledge and skills to address immediate needs and long-term goals.

Improvisation is rooted in principles that encourage openness, collaboration, and a willingness to experiment. In practice, it involves creating an environment where employees feel empowered to make decisions and take actions without waiting for detailed instructions or approvals. This requires a culture of trust and psychological safety, where team members are confident that their contributions are valued and that mistakes are seen as opportunities for learning rather than failures.

Agility in organizational settings is closely linked to the concept of iterative development, where processes and products are continuously improved through cycles of feedback and refinement. This approach allows organizations to remain responsive to change, as each iteration provides new insights and opportunities for enhancement. Improvisation complements this by enabling rapid adjustments and innovations during each cycle, ensuring that the organization can respond effectively to emerging trends and challenges.

Leadership plays a vital role in fostering an environment conducive to improvisation and agile responses. Leaders must encourage a mindset of flexibility and adaptability, promoting a culture that embraces change rather than fearing it. By providing the necessary resources, support, and autonomy, leaders can empower their teams to think creatively and act swiftly in the face of uncertainty.

Improvisation also benefits from cross-functional collaboration, where diverse teams bring different perspectives and expertise to the table. This diversity enhances the ability to generate innovative ideas and solutions, as team members can draw on a wide range of experiences and knowledge. Encouraging open communication and collaboration across departments breaks down silos and promotes a more integrated approach to problem-solving.

Technology plays a significant role in supporting improvisation and agility. Advanced tools and platforms facilitate real-time communication, collaboration, and data analysis, enabling teams to make informed decisions quickly. Technology also provides access to a wealth of information and resources, further enhancing the capacity for improvisation.

Embracing improvisation and agile response to change is essential for organizations aiming to thrive in today's dynamic business landscape. By fostering a culture of flexibility, trust, and collaboration, and by leveraging the power of technology, organizations can enhance their ability to innovate and adapt swiftly. This approach not only improves immediate problem-solving capabilities but also builds long-term resilience and competitive advantage.

Case studies of innovation through improvisation highlight the significant impact that spontaneous and creative problem-solving can have on organizational success. One notable example is the development of the Post-it Note by 3M. Initially, 3M scientist Spencer Silver was attempting to create a super-strong adhesive but instead ended up with a low-tack adhesive. Rather than discarding this unexpected result, Silver and his colleague Art Fry improvised by finding a practical application for it. Fry realized that this adhesive could be used to create bookmarks that would stick temporarily to paper without leaving residue. This improvisation led to the creation of the now-iconic Post-it Note, demonstrating how flexibility and openness to new ideas can lead to groundbreaking products.

Another example is the pivot made by Slack, the popular collaboration tool. Slack started as an internal communication tool for a gaming company called Tiny Speck. When the original game project failed to gain traction, the team improvised by shifting their focus to the internal tool they had developed. Recognizing its potential value to other organizations, they refined and marketed it as a standalone product. This agile response to a business failure resulted in one of the most widely used collaboration platforms in the world, illustrating the power of improvisation in redirecting efforts towards more promising opportunities.

Airbnb's origin story also exemplifies innovation through improvisation. The company's founders, Brian Chesky and Joe Gebbia, were struggling to pay rent and decided to rent out air mattresses in their apartment during a conference when hotel rooms were scarce. This impromptu solution to their financial problem led them to realize the potential of a peer-to-peer lodging platform. They improvised by creating a website to facilitate bookings, which eventually evolved into the global hospitality service Airbnb. This case underscores how improvisation in response to immediate needs can uncover significant business opportunities.

Netflix provides another compelling case of improvisation leading to innovation. Originally a DVD rental service, Netflix faced the threat of obsolescence with the rise of digital streaming. Rather than sticking to their original business model, Netflix improvised by transitioning to an online streaming service. They further innovated by producing original content, which has become a major component of their strategy. This ability to pivot and adapt has positioned Netflix as a leader in the entertainment industry, demonstrating the importance of flexibility and creative problem-solving.

Tesla's approach to product development and innovation also reflects the principles of improvisation. Faced with the challenge of creating an electric vehicle that could compete with traditional gasoline cars, Tesla continuously iterated on their designs and technology. They took risks by incorporating cutting-edge technology and responded to market feedback with agility. This iterative process, driven by a willingness to experiment and adapt, has enabled Tesla to lead the electric vehicle market.

These case studies illustrate that improvisation is a powerful tool for fostering innovation. By remaining open to unexpected outcomes, embracing flexibility, and being willing to pivot when necessary, organizations can uncover new opportunities and achieve remarkable success. Improvisation not only helps in navigating immediate challenges but also fosters a culture of creativity and resilience, positioning organizations to thrive in an ever-changing business landscape.

Building a culture of innovation requires creating an environment where creativity and experimentation are encouraged and supported at all levels of the organization. This begins with leadership setting the tone by demonstrating a commitment to innovation and fostering an atmosphere that values new ideas and risk-taking. Leaders must model innovative behaviors, provide resources and support for creative initiatives, and recognize and reward innovative efforts. By doing so, they signal to the rest of the organization that innovation is a priority and that it is safe to take risks and experiment.

Open communication is crucial for fostering innovation. Organizations should encourage the free flow of ideas and ensure that employees feel comfortable sharing their thoughts without fear of criticism or retribution. This can be achieved through regular brainstorming sessions, idea-sharing platforms, and creating spaces where informal discussions and collaborations can occur. Encouraging cross-functional teams and diverse perspectives can also lead to more innovative solutions, as employees from different backgrounds and areas of expertise bring unique viewpoints to the table.

Providing employees with the time and resources to pursue innovative projects is another key element. This can involve allocating specific time for creative thinking and experimentation, such as Google's well-known "20% time" policy, which allows employees to spend a portion of their workweek on projects outside their regular responsibilities. Access to necessary tools, technology, and training also empowers employees to develop and implement new ideas effectively.

Recognizing and rewarding innovation helps reinforce its importance within the organizational culture. Celebrating successes, whether through formal recognition programs, awards, or public acknowledgment, can motivate employees to continue contributing creative ideas. It's also important to recognize the effort and learning involved in unsuccessful attempts, as these experiences provide valuable insights and can lead to future innovations.

Embedding innovation into the organizational processes and structures can further support a culture of creativity. This might include integrating innovation goals into performance evaluations, establishing dedicated innovation teams or labs, and incorporating innovation metrics into the organization's overall performance indicators. By embedding innovation into the fabric of the organization, it becomes a sustained and integral part of how the organization operates.

Continuous learning and development are vital for maintaining a culture of innovation. Organizations should provide opportunities for employees to enhance their skills and knowledge through training, workshops, conferences, and access to online learning resources. Encouraging a growth mindset, where employees see challenges as opportunities to learn and grow, can further support a culture of continuous improvement and innovation.

Building a culture of innovation also involves creating an inclusive environment where diverse perspectives are valued and leveraged. Diversity in thought and experience can lead to more creative solutions and help organizations better understand and meet the needs of a diverse customer base. Ensuring that all employees feel included and respected, and that their contributions are valued, can drive higher levels of engagement and innovation.

Creating innovative organizations requires a holistic approach that includes leadership commitment, open communication, dedicated time and resources for creative projects, recognition and rewards for innovative efforts, embedding innovation into organizational processes, fostering continuous learning, and promoting diversity and inclusion. By nurturing these elements, organizations can create an environment where innovation thrives, leading to sustained growth, adaptability, and competitive advantage in a rapidly changing business landscape.

In Chapter 3, we explored the vital role of creativity and improvisation in fostering organizational innovation. We began by discussing the fundamental importance of creativity within organizations, highlighting how it serves as the foundation for generating new and valuable ideas that drive competitive advantage. Encouraging creativity involves fostering an environment that supports experimentation, values diverse perspectives, and promotes interdisciplinary collaboration.

We then delved into the concept of improvisation and its significance in enabling agile responses to change. Unlike traditional, rigid approaches, improvisation emphasizes flexibility, adaptability, and quick decision-making, allowing organizations to navigate unexpected challenges and seize new opportunities effectively. By embracing improvisational techniques, organizations can enhance their ability to innovate and respond to dynamic market conditions.

Through various case studies, we illustrated how organizations like 3M, Slack, Airbnb, Netflix, and Tesla have successfully leveraged improvisation to drive innovation. These examples underscored the power of flexibility and creative problem-solving in achieving remarkable success and maintaining a competitive edge. We also discussed how to build a culture of innovation within an organization. This involves leadership commitment, open communication, providing resources for creative projects, recognizing and rewarding innovation, embedding innovation into organizational processes, fostering continuous learning, and promoting diversity and inclusion. By nurturing these elements, organizations can create an environment where innovation thrives and becomes an integral part of the organizational DNA.

It is essential to recognize that fostering a culture of innovation is an ongoing journey that requires continuous effort and commitment. By embracing creativity and improvisation, and by building a supportive environment for innovation, organizations can enhance their resilience, adaptability, and long-term success. This chapter has provided you with insights and practical strategies to inspire and implement innovative practices within your organization.

The next chapters will build on these foundational concepts, exploring advanced methodologies and future directions in organizational development. Together, we will continue to uncover the tools and techniques necessary to lead your organization through the complexities of change and towards a thriving, innovative future. Let the principles of creativity and improvisation guide you as you embark on this transformative journey, unlocking new potentials and driving your organization to greater heights.

Chapter 4: Organizational Strategy and Learning

In Chapter 4 we explore the intricate relationship between organizational strategy and learning, exploring how continuous learning and strategic alignment can drive sustained competitive advantage. This chapter provides a comprehensive overview of the theories and models that underpin organizational learning and examines how these concepts can be integrated into strategic planning to foster a culture of continuous improvement and adaptation.

Theories and models of organizational learning form the foundation of our understanding of how organizations acquire, disseminate, and apply knowledge. These theories explain the processes through which organizations learn from their experiences, both successes and failures, and how they can use this knowledge to improve performance and innovate. We will explore key theories, including those proposed by notable scholars like Chris Argyris, Donald Schön, and Peter Senge, whose work has significantly shaped our understanding of organizational learning.

Resource-based and knowledge-based views of the firm offer valuable perspectives on how internal resources and knowledge assets contribute to competitive advantage. The resource-based view (RBV) emphasizes the strategic importance of developing unique resources and capabilities that are valuable, rare, inimitable, and non-substitutable. Meanwhile, the knowledge-based view (KBV) focuses on the critical role of knowledge creation, sharing, and utilization within the organization. Understanding these views helps organizations leverage their internal strengths to achieve and sustain competitive advantage.

The dynamic capabilities framework builds on the RBV and KBV, emphasizing the need for organizations to continuously integrate, build, and reconfigure internal and external competencies to address rapidly changing environments. This framework highlights three main capacities: sensing opportunities and threats, seizing opportunities, and transforming the organization to maintain competitiveness. By developing dynamic capabilities, organizations can enhance their agility and responsiveness to market changes.

Aligning organizational strategy with learning practices ensures that learning activities directly support strategic objectives. This alignment is crucial for fostering an environment where continuous improvement is part of the organizational culture. We will discuss strategies for integrating learning into strategic planning processes, ensuring that knowledge development and utilization are closely linked to achieving organizational goals.

Continuous improvement and adaptation are essential for long-term success in a constantly changing business environment. Organizations must foster a culture of continuous learning, where employees at all levels are encouraged to seek out new knowledge, experiment with new approaches, and learn from their experiences. This chapter will explore methods for embedding continuous improvement into the organizational fabric, ensuring that the organization remains adaptable and resilient in the face of change.

By the end of this chapter, you will have a deeper understanding of the critical relationship between organizational strategy and learning. You will be equipped with practical insights and strategies to foster a culture of continuous learning and improvement, aligning your organization's strategic objectives with its learning activities. This alignment is key to navigating the complexities of today's business environment and achieving sustained success.

Theories and models of organizational learning provide a framework for understanding how organizations acquire, share, and apply knowledge to improve performance and foster innovation. One foundational concept in this area is the single-loop and double-loop learning theory proposed by Chris Argyris and Donald Schön. Single-loop learning involves making adjustments based on feedback to correct errors without questioning underlying assumptions. In contrast, double-loop learning involves reflecting on and challenging these assumptions, leading to more profound and transformative changes in behavior and practices.

Peter Senge's concept of the learning organization, introduced in his book "The Fifth Discipline," emphasizes the importance of continuous learning and adaptation. Senge identifies five disciplines that are essential for creating a learning organization: systems thinking, personal mastery, mental models, shared vision, and team learning. Systems thinking helps organizations understand the interrelationships between different parts of the system. Personal mastery encourages individuals to continuously improve their skills and capabilities. Mental models involve recognizing and challenging ingrained assumptions and beliefs. Shared vision aligns the organization's goals and aspirations, while team learning fosters collective problem-solving and innovation.

Nonaka and Takeuchi's knowledge creation model, also known as the SECI model, outlines the dynamic process of knowledge conversion within organizations. This model describes four modes of knowledge conversion: socialization, externalization, combination, and internalization. Socialization involves sharing tacit knowledge through direct interaction and observation. Externalization is the process of articulating tacit knowledge into explicit concepts. Combination involves integrating different pieces of explicit knowledge into a more complex system. Internalization is the process of absorbing explicit knowledge into tacit knowledge through practice and experience.

Levitt and March's model of organizational learning focuses on the role of routines and standard operating procedures in learning. According to this model, organizations learn by encoding inferences from history into routines that guide behavior. This process helps organizations retain and institutionalize knowledge, allowing them to replicate successful practices and avoid past mistakes. However, reliance on routines can also lead to rigidity and inhibit innovation if not periodically reviewed and updated.

The 4I Framework, developed by Crossan, Lane, and White, highlights the multilevel nature of organizational learning, encompassing individual, group, and organizational levels. This framework identifies four processes: intuiting, interpreting, integrating, and institutionalizing. Intuiting is the recognition of patterns and possibilities at the individual level. Interpreting involves explaining and sharing insights with others. Integrating is the process of developing shared understanding and coordinated actions. Institutionalizing embeds learning into the organization's systems, structures, and routines.

These theories and models of organizational learning provide valuable insights into how organizations can foster a culture of continuous improvement and adaptability. By understanding and applying these concepts, organizations can enhance their ability to learn from experience, innovate, and respond effectively to changing environments. Embracing a holistic approach to learning that encompasses individual, group, and organizational levels is essential for achieving sustained success and competitive advantage.

The resource-based view (RBV) and the knowledge-based view (KBV) are two influential perspectives that explain how organizations achieve and sustain competitive advantage through their internal resources and capabilities. The resource-based view emphasizes the importance of developing and managing resources that are valuable, rare, inimitable, and non-substitutable. These resources can include tangible assets like technology and infrastructure, as well as intangible assets like brand reputation, intellectual property, and organizational culture. By focusing on cultivating these unique resources, organizations can create barriers to imitation and build a sustainable competitive advantage.

According to the RBV, the strategic management of resources involves identifying and leveraging the organization's core competencies. These are the collective learning and capabilities that enable the organization to perform better than its competitors. Core competencies should be continually developed and protected to maintain their value. For example, a company with a strong research and development team may leverage its innovation capabilities to stay ahead in the market. The RBV highlights the internal factors that contribute to competitive success and underscores the need for organizations to invest in their unique strengths.

The knowledge-based view extends the resource-based perspective by emphasizing that knowledge is the most strategically significant resource of an organization. Knowledge assets, such as expertise, skills, and intellectual capital, are critical drivers of innovation and performance. The KBV posits that the ability to create, share, and apply knowledge effectively within the organization is a key determinant of competitive advantage. Knowledge is often embedded in the routines, processes, and practices of the organization, making it difficult for competitors to replicate.

Knowledge creation and management are central to the KBV. Organizations must develop processes for generating new knowledge, such as research and development, experimentation, and learning from experience. Sharing knowledge across the organization is also crucial, as it ensures that valuable insights and expertise are accessible to all members. This can be facilitated through collaborative tools, training programs, and knowledge-sharing platforms. The application of knowledge involves using insights and information to improve decision-making, innovate, and solve problems.

The KBV also emphasizes the role of dynamic capabilities in maintaining a competitive edge. Dynamic capabilities are the organization's ability to integrate, build, and reconfigure internal and external competences to address rapidly changing environments. These capabilities involve sensing opportunities and threats, seizing opportunities, and transforming the organization to stay aligned with the external context. By continuously renewing their knowledge base and adapting to change, organizations can remain resilient and competitive.

Together, the resource-based and knowledge-based views provide a comprehensive understanding of how organizations can achieve long-term success. The RBV focuses on leveraging unique resources and capabilities, while the KBV highlights the strategic importance of knowledge and the processes for managing it. By integrating these perspectives, organizations can develop robust strategies that capitalize on their internal strengths and foster continuous innovation and adaptability. This holistic approach enables organizations to build and sustain competitive advantage in a complex and dynamic business environment.

The dynamic capabilities framework is an extension of the resource-based and knowledge-based views, focusing on an organization's ability to adapt, renew, and reconfigure its resources and competences in response to rapidly changing environments. This framework emphasizes the importance of developing capabilities that enable organizations to sense opportunities and threats, seize opportunities, and transform their operations to maintain competitiveness.

Sensing involves the ability to identify and assess external opportunities and threats. This capability requires organizations to constantly scan the environment, gather relevant information, and interpret market trends and technological advancements. Effective sensing allows organizations to stay ahead of changes and anticipate shifts in consumer preferences, competitive actions, and regulatory developments.

Seizing refers to the ability to mobilize resources and capture value from identified opportunities. Once an opportunity is sensed, organizations need to act swiftly to capitalize on it. This involves making strategic decisions, allocating resources, and implementing new processes, products, or services. Seizing opportunities often requires significant investment in innovation, marketing, and infrastructure to ensure successful execution.

Transforming is the capability to continuously realign and reconfigure the organization's structure, culture, and operations to adapt to new conditions. Transformation ensures that the organization remains agile and resilient, capable of responding effectively to internal and external changes. This capability involves reshaping business models, processes, and practices to sustain long-term growth and competitiveness. It often requires fostering a culture of continuous improvement and learning, where employees are encouraged to embrace change and contribute to the organization's evolution.

The dynamic capabilities framework highlights the importance of agility and adaptability in maintaining a competitive edge. Organizations with strong dynamic capabilities can navigate uncertainty and complexity more effectively than those relying solely on static resources and competences. Developing these capabilities requires a commitment to innovation, strategic foresight, and organizational flexibility.

Leadership plays a crucial role in building and nurturing dynamic capabilities. Leaders must champion a vision of agility and adaptability, encouraging a proactive approach to change. They should invest in the development of skills and competences that support dynamic capabilities, such as strategic thinking, decision-making, and change management. Additionally, leaders need to create an environment that fosters collaboration, knowledge sharing, and continuous learning.

The dynamic capabilities framework underscores the importance of continuous renewal and adaptation. In a rapidly evolving business landscape, organizations cannot rely on past successes or static advantages. Instead, they must develop the ability to sense opportunities and threats, seize opportunities swiftly, and transform their operations to stay competitive. This approach ensures that organizations remain resilient, innovative, and capable of sustaining long-term success in a dynamic environment. By integrating the principles of the dynamic capabilities framework, organizations can enhance their strategic agility and maintain a robust competitive position.

Aligning strategy with organizational learning is crucial for fostering an environment where continuous improvement and adaptability are part of the organizational culture. This alignment ensures that learning activities directly support the strategic objectives of the organization, enhancing its capacity to innovate, respond to changes, and achieve long-term success.

One of the first steps in aligning strategy with learning is integrating learning and development into the strategic planning process. This involves identifying the skills and knowledge required to achieve strategic goals and developing targeted learning initiatives to build these capabilities. By doing so, organizations can ensure that their workforce is equipped with the competencies needed to execute the strategy effectively.

Organizations should also establish a strategic learning agenda that outlines the specific learning priorities and objectives aligned with their strategic goals. This agenda should be regularly reviewed and updated to reflect changing strategic priorities and emerging challenges. It helps to create a clear link between learning activities and strategic outcomes, ensuring that learning efforts are focused and impactful.

Another important aspect is fostering a culture of continuous learning and improvement. Organizations can achieve this by encouraging employees to seek out new knowledge, experiment with new approaches, and learn from their experiences. Leaders play a crucial role in modeling these behaviors and creating an environment where learning is valued and supported. Providing opportunities for employees to share their knowledge and collaborate on problem-solving can further enhance organizational learning.

Measurement and evaluation are essential for ensuring that learning initiatives are aligned with strategic objectives.

Organizations should establish clear metrics to assess the impact of learning activities on performance and strategic outcomes. Regular evaluations help track progress, identify areas for improvement, and ensure that learning initiatives remain relevant and effective. Feedback loops should be created to gather insights from employees and adjust learning programs as needed.

Embedding learning into the daily operations of the organization ensures that it becomes a natural part of how work is conducted. This can be achieved through mechanisms such as learning communities, mentorship programs, and on-the-job training. By integrating learning into routine activities, organizations can create a continuous cycle of knowledge acquisition and application.

Leadership commitment is vital for aligning strategy with organizational learning. Leaders must prioritize learning and development, allocate necessary resources, and champion learning initiatives. They should communicate the strategic importance of learning to the organization and ensure that it is embedded in the organizational values and practices.

Aligning strategy with organizational learning involves integrating learning into strategic planning, establishing a strategic learning agenda, fostering a culture of continuous improvement, measuring the impact of learning activities, embedding learning into daily operations, and securing leadership commitment. This alignment enhances an organization's ability to adapt, innovate, and achieve sustained success in a rapidly changing business environment. By prioritizing learning and ensuring it supports strategic goals, organizations can build a resilient and agile workforce capable of driving long-term performance and growth.

Continuous improvement and adaptation are vital for an organization's long-term success and resilience in a constantly changing environment. These processes involve the ongoing effort to enhance products, services, and processes by making incremental improvements and significant innovations. By fostering a culture of continuous improvement, organizations can remain agile and responsive to new challenges and opportunities.

Creating a culture of continuous improvement starts with encouraging a mindset of constant learning and development among employees. This involves promoting the idea that there is always room for improvement and that everyone in the organization can contribute to this process. Leaders play a crucial role by modeling this mindset and providing opportunities for employees to learn, experiment, and innovate. They should encourage employees to question existing practices, propose new ideas, and share their insights openly.

Feedback is a critical component of continuous improvement. Organizations should establish mechanisms for regularly collecting and analyzing feedback from various sources, including employees, customers, and other stakeholders. This feedback provides valuable insights into areas that need improvement and helps identify emerging trends and issues. By acting on this feedback, organizations can make informed decisions and implement changes that enhance their performance and effectiveness.

Adaptation involves the ability to adjust strategies, processes, and operations in response to changing external conditions. This requires a proactive approach to monitoring the external environment and anticipating potential disruptions and opportunities. Organizations need to be flexible and willing to pivot when necessary, reallocating resources and adjusting plans to stay aligned with their strategic objectives. This flexibility enables organizations to respond swiftly to market changes, technological advancements, and evolving customer needs.

Continuous improvement and adaptation also involve leveraging data and analytics to drive decision-making. By using data to identify patterns, measure performance, and predict future trends, organizations can make more informed and effective decisions. This data-driven approach helps organizations prioritize improvement initiatives, track progress, and evaluate the impact of changes.

Collaboration and knowledge sharing are essential for fostering continuous improvement and adaptation. Organizations should create an environment where employees feel empowered to collaborate across functions and share their knowledge and expertise. This cross-functional collaboration can lead to more innovative solutions and ensure that improvements are integrated throughout the organization.

Training and development programs are crucial for equipping employees with the skills and knowledge needed to contribute to continuous improvement efforts. These programs should focus not only on technical skills but also on critical thinking, problem-solving, and creativity. By investing in employee development, organizations can build a capable and motivated workforce that drives ongoing improvement and innovation.

Leadership support is vital for sustaining continuous improvement and adaptation. Leaders must champion these efforts, provide the necessary resources, and create an environment that encourages experimentation and learning. They should recognize and reward employees who contribute to improvement initiatives, reinforcing the importance of continuous improvement as a core organizational value.

Continuous improvement and adaptation are essential for maintaining organizational agility and resilience. By fostering a culture of constant learning, leveraging feedback and data, promoting collaboration, investing in employee development, and securing leadership support, organizations can enhance their ability to adapt to change and continuously improve their performance. This approach ensures that organizations remain competitive and capable of thriving in a dynamic business landscape.

In Chapter 4, we have explored the intricate relationship between organizational strategy and learning, emphasizing how continuous learning and strategic alignment drive sustained competitive advantage. We began by examining key theories and models of organizational learning, such as single-loop and double-loop learning, the concept of the learning organization, the SECI model, and the 4I Framework. These theories provide a robust foundation for understanding how organizations can effectively acquire, share, and apply knowledge to enhance performance and foster innovation.

We then delved into the resource-based and knowledge-based views, which highlight the importance of leveraging unique resources and knowledge assets to achieve and sustain competitive advantage. The dynamic capabilities framework extended these perspectives by emphasizing the need for organizations to develop capabilities that enable them to sense opportunities and threats, seize opportunities, and transform their operations to remain competitive in rapidly changing environments.

Aligning organizational strategy with learning was also a key focus, where we discussed integrating learning into strategic planning, establishing a strategic learning agenda, fostering a culture of continuous improvement, measuring the impact of learning activities, embedding learning into daily operations, and securing leadership commitment. This alignment ensures that learning initiatives directly support strategic objectives, enhancing the organization's ability to innovate, respond to changes, and achieve long-term success.

We concluded with a discussion on continuous improvement and adaptation, highlighting the importance of fostering a culture of constant learning and development, leveraging feedback and data, promoting collaboration, investing in employee development, and securing leadership support. These processes are vital for maintaining organizational agility and resilience, enabling organizations to remain competitive and capable of thriving in a dynamic business landscape.

As we move forward in this book, remember that the principles of organizational learning and strategic alignment are not static concepts but dynamic processes that require ongoing commitment and adaptation. By embracing these principles, you can build a resilient and agile organization that is well-equipped to navigate the complexities of the modern business environment. Let the insights and strategies discussed in this chapter inspire you to foster a culture of continuous learning and improvement, driving your organization toward sustained success and growth. Through dedication and a proactive approach to learning and adaptation, you can lead your organization to achieve its strategic goals and thrive in an ever-evolving world.

Chapter 5: Social Network Analysis

In the contemporary organizational landscape, understanding the intricate web of relationships and interactions among employees is crucial for fostering effective communication, driving innovation, and enhancing leadership. Chapter 5 delves into the concept of Social Network Analysis (SNA), a powerful tool that allows organizations to map and analyze the informal networks that significantly influence organizational dynamics and performance.

Informal networks, often invisible yet highly influential, comprise the spontaneous, organic connections that form outside the formal organizational structure. These networks can include friendships, mentorships, and collaborative relationships that are not officially recognized on organizational charts but play a crucial role in the flow of information and resources.

The importance of social networks in organizations cannot be overstated. These networks facilitate information exchange, support collaboration, and often act as conduits for innovation. They influence decision-making processes and the dissemination of knowledge, ultimately impacting organizational efficiency and effectiveness. By understanding these networks, leaders can identify key influencers, uncover hidden bottlenecks, and foster a more cohesive and productive organizational environment.

To effectively leverage social networks, organizations need tools and methods for Social Network Analysis. SNA involves the use of various techniques to collect, visualize, and analyze data on the relationships within an organization. This can include surveys, interviews, and digital communication logs, which are then used to create network maps that highlight the connections and interactions between individuals. These visualizations can reveal critical insights into how information flows and where potential improvements can be made.

Applications of Social Network Analysis are vast and varied. In communication, SNA can identify how information circulates and highlight areas where communication may be lacking. In innovation, understanding social networks can help organizations foster environments where creative ideas are more likely to emerge and spread. In leadership, SNA can identify key influencers and informal leaders who can drive change initiatives and enhance overall organizational effectiveness.

As we explore Social Network Analysis in this chapter, you will gain a deeper understanding of how to harness the power of informal networks to improve communication, spur innovation, and strengthen leadership within your organization. By leveraging SNA, you can uncover the hidden dynamics that drive organizational success and create strategies that align these networks with your strategic goals. This chapter will equip you with the knowledge and tools to transform your understanding of organizational relationships and enhance your ability to lead in a connected, networked world.

Informal networks within organizations are the spontaneous and organic connections that form outside the formal structure. These networks consist of relationships and interactions that are not officially recognized on organizational charts but are vital for the flow of information, collaboration, and support among employees. Unlike formal networks, which are defined by hierarchical lines of authority and prescribed roles, informal networks emerge naturally based on shared interests, mutual trust, and personal interactions.

These networks play a crucial role in how work actually gets done within an organization. They facilitate the exchange of information and knowledge that might not flow through formal channels, often speeding up processes and enabling quicker problem-solving. Informal networks also foster collaboration across different departments and levels of the organization, breaking down silos and encouraging a more integrated approach to achieving organizational goals.

Understanding informal networks involves recognizing the various types of connections that can exist. These can include friendships, mentorships, and informal peer support groups. Each of these connections contributes to the overall dynamic of the organization, influencing morale, productivity, and innovation. Friendships provide emotional support and a sense of belonging, which can enhance job satisfaction and retention. Mentorships offer guidance and career development, helping employees navigate their professional paths more effectively. Informal peer support groups create a space for sharing best practices and troubleshooting issues collaboratively.

Identifying and analyzing these networks can provide valuable insights into the real workings of an organization. Social Network Analysis (SNA) is a tool used to map and measure these informal relationships, revealing the true web of interactions. Through SNA, organizations can visualize how employees are connected, identify key influencers, and understand the flow of information. This analysis can uncover bottlenecks where communication is hindered and highlight areas where fostering more connections could lead to greater innovation and efficiency.

By understanding informal networks, leaders can better leverage these connections to enhance organizational performance. For example, they can identify and support key influencers who can help drive change initiatives and ensure that important information reaches all parts of the organization. Additionally, recognizing the importance of informal networks can lead to more targeted efforts to improve employee engagement and collaboration. Leaders can create opportunities for informal interactions through team-building activities, cross-functional projects, and social events.

Overall, informal networks are a critical but often overlooked aspect of organizational life. They provide the social infrastructure that supports formal processes and structures, contributing significantly to an organization's ability to function effectively. By paying attention to these networks and understanding their dynamics, organizations can enhance their internal communication, foster innovation, and improve overall performance. Recognizing the value of informal networks and strategically nurturing them can lead to a more connected, cohesive, and resilient organization.

Social networks in organizations are essential for the flow of information, the sharing of knowledge, and the fostering of collaboration. These networks, which consist of informal connections and relationships among employees, play a critical role in the overall functioning and success of an organization. By facilitating communication, they help ensure that important information reaches the right people promptly, enabling quicker decision-making and problem-solving. These networks often operate alongside formal structures, providing a complementary pathway for the dissemination of ideas and information.

The importance of social networks extends to innovation and creativity within organizations. Informal networks enable employees to share insights and brainstorm ideas in a less structured environment, which can lead to more creative solutions and innovative thinking. When people from different departments and backgrounds interact, they bring diverse perspectives that can spark new ideas and drive innovation. These interactions often happen spontaneously in informal settings, such as during breaks, at social events, or through casual conversations, making social networks a vital incubator for innovation.

Social networks also significantly impact employee engagement and morale. Strong, positive connections among employees can create a sense of community and belonging, which enhances job satisfaction and reduces turnover. When employees feel connected to their colleagues, they are more likely to be motivated, committed, and productive. Social networks provide emotional and professional support, helping employees navigate challenges and stay resilient in the face of difficulties.

In terms of influence and power dynamics, social networks reveal the informal power structures within an organization. Not all influential figures hold formal leadership positions; some derive their influence from their ability to connect with others and mobilize resources through their social networks. Identifying these key influencers can be crucial for effective change management and leadership. Leveraging the influence of these informal leaders can help drive initiatives and ensure broader acceptance and participation across the organization.

Team and organizational performance are also closely linked to the quality of social networks. Cohesive networks enhance trust, cooperation, and coordination among team members, leading to better performance and outcomes. Conversely, fragmented networks with isolated groups can hinder collaboration and communication, negatively impacting performance. Understanding the structure and health of social networks allows organizations to address gaps and strengthen connections where needed.

Social networks play a vital role in knowledge sharing. They enable the transfer of tacit knowledge, which is often unrecorded and resides in the experiences and insights of employees. This type of knowledge is shared more effectively through personal interactions and informal communication channels. By promoting strong social networks, organizations can ensure that valuable knowledge is passed on and utilized, contributing to continuous learning and improvement. These networks are a critical component of organizational life. They enhance communication, foster innovation, support employee engagement, reveal informal power dynamics, improve performance, and facilitate knowledge sharing. Recognizing and nurturing these networks can lead to a more dynamic, resilient, and successful organization. By understanding the importance of social networks, leaders can create strategies to strengthen these connections and harness their full potential for the benefit of the organization.

Social Network Analysis (SNA) employs a variety of tools and methods to map and measure the relationships and flows between people, groups, and organizations. These tools help visualize and understand the structure and dynamics of informal networks within an organization, providing insights into how information and influence move through these networks.

One primary method used in SNA is data collection through surveys and questionnaires. These tools ask employees to identify their connections within the organization, including who they communicate with, seek advice from, or collaborate with regularly. The data gathered from these surveys provide the foundational information needed to construct a network map.

Observation and interviews are also valuable methods for collecting data on social networks. By observing interactions and conducting in-depth interviews, analysts can gain qualitative insights into the nature and strength of relationships. This approach helps capture the nuances of informal networks that might not be apparent through surveys alone.

Once data is collected, specialized software tools are used to create visual representations of the networks. Programs like UCINET, Gephi, and NodeXL enable analysts to generate network diagrams that illustrate the connections between individuals. These visualizations, often called sociograms, use nodes to represent individuals and edges to represent the relationships between them. Different colors, sizes, and shapes can be used to denote various attributes and the strength of connections, providing a clear picture of the network's structure.

Centrality measures are crucial in SNA for identifying key players within the network. These measures include degree centrality, which counts the number of direct connections an individual has; betweenness centrality, which identifies individuals who act as bridges or connectors between different parts of the network; and closeness centrality, which measures how quickly an individual can reach all other nodes in the network. These metrics help pinpoint influential individuals and potential bottlenecks in the flow of information.

Cluster analysis is another method used in SNA to identify groups or communities within the network. This technique detects subgroups of nodes that are more densely connected to each other than to the rest of the network. Understanding these clusters can reveal insights into subcultures, collaboration patterns, and potential areas for improving connectivity.

Sentiment analysis can be integrated with SNA to understand the tone and quality of interactions within the network. By analyzing communication content, such as emails or social media exchanges, sentiment analysis tools can provide additional context about the nature of relationships and the overall health of the network. Positive, supportive interactions can indicate strong, healthy networks, while negative or conflicted interactions might signal areas needing attention.

Longitudinal analysis involves studying network changes over time. By conducting SNA at multiple points, organizations can track how their social networks evolve, assess the impact of interventions, and understand trends in relationships and communication patterns. This dynamic perspective is essential for continuous improvement and adaptation.

Ethnographic methods can complement traditional SNA by providing a deeper, contextual understanding of the social networks within an organization. Through immersive observation and participation, ethnographers can capture the cultural and social nuances that influence network formation and operation, offering richer insights into the human aspects of organizational life.

Tools and methods for Social Network Analysis, including surveys, observations, specialized software, centrality measures, cluster analysis, sentiment analysis, longitudinal studies, and ethnographic methods, enable organizations to map, visualize, and understand their informal networks. By leveraging these tools, organizations can gain valuable insights into the flow of information, influence, and collaboration, ultimately enhancing communication, innovation, and overall performance.

Social Network Analysis (SNA) has a wide range of applications in communication, innovation, and leadership within organizations. In communication, SNA helps identify how information flows through the organization, pinpointing central figures who act as key conduits of information. Understanding these pathways allows organizations to optimize communication channels, ensuring that critical information reaches all necessary parties efficiently. It can also reveal communication bottlenecks or silos that may hinder effective information dissemination, enabling targeted interventions to improve connectivity and reduce barriers.

In the realm of innovation, SNA can identify clusters of individuals who frequently collaborate and exchange ideas, highlighting potential innovation hubs within the organization. By understanding these informal networks, organizations can foster environments that encourage creativity and the cross-pollination of ideas. SNA can also identify individuals who bridge different groups, known as boundary spanners, who can facilitate the transfer of innovative ideas across various parts of the organization. Encouraging and supporting these individuals can enhance the organization's overall innovative capacity.

Leadership applications of SNA involve identifying informal leaders who exert significant influence over their peers, regardless of their formal position within the organization. These individuals often play crucial roles in shaping the organization's culture and driving change initiatives. By recognizing and engaging these key influencers, formal leaders can more effectively promote new initiatives and gain broader acceptance across the organization. Additionally, SNA can help in succession planning by highlighting emerging leaders who possess strong networks and influence, ensuring a smooth transition of leadership roles.

SNA also aids in understanding the social dynamics that affect employee engagement and morale. By mapping out social connections, organizations can identify isolated employees or groups that may be at risk of disengagement. Interventions can then be designed to integrate these individuals more fully into the organizational fabric, fostering a more inclusive and supportive environment. This can lead to higher levels of job satisfaction and retention.

In change management, SNA provides insights into how change-related information and attitudes are spreading through the organization. By tracking the influence of key nodes within the network, leaders can address resistance more effectively and support change agents who facilitate the adoption of new practices. This understanding helps in tailoring communication strategies to ensure they are more impactful and aligned with the organization's social structure.

SNA can be used to enhance team performance by understanding the internal dynamics and interactions within teams. By analyzing these relationships, organizations can form more cohesive and effective teams, optimize roles based on existing connections, and improve collaboration. This leads to better decision-making and more efficient project execution.

The applications of Social Network Analysis in communication, innovation, and leadership are extensive and impactful. By mapping and analyzing the informal networks within an organization, SNA provides valuable insights that enhance information flow, foster innovation, identify and support key influencers, improve employee engagement, facilitate effective change management, and optimize team dynamics. These applications collectively contribute to a more dynamic, responsive, and high-performing organization.

We have explored the essential role of Social Network Analysis (SNA) in understanding and leveraging informal networks within organizations. These networks, although often unseen in formal organizational charts, are critical to the flow of information, innovation, and leadership dynamics.

We began by exploring the concept of informal networks, highlighting their spontaneous and organic nature. These networks facilitate essential interactions that drive organizational performance and employee engagement, making them indispensable to understanding how work truly gets done.

The importance of social networks in organizations cannot be overstated. They are pivotal for effective communication, fostering innovation, enhancing employee engagement, and revealing informal power structures. By recognizing and nurturing these networks, organizations can improve overall efficiency, support a more cohesive work environment, and drive continuous improvement.

Tools and methods for Social Network Analysis, such as surveys, interviews, observation, and specialized software, provide the means to visualize and analyze these intricate webs of relationships. Techniques like centrality measures, cluster analysis, sentiment analysis, and longitudinal studies help organizations identify key influencers, understand network health, and track changes over time. These tools offer a comprehensive understanding of how social networks function and how they can be optimized.

The applications of SNA in communication, innovation, and leadership demonstrate its wide-reaching impact. In communication, SNA helps identify key information conduits and eliminate bottlenecks. For innovation, it highlights collaboration hubs and boundary spanners who drive creative solutions. In leadership, it identifies informal leaders and key influencers who can be leveraged to drive organizational change and foster a positive culture.

By applying SNA, organizations can gain profound insights into their informal networks, leading to better communication strategies, enhanced innovation processes, and more effective leadership. Understanding and harnessing the power of these networks can result in a more agile, innovative, and resilient organization.

As we conclude this chapter, it is essential to recognize that the power of SNA lies not only in its ability to map relationships but also in its capacity to inform strategic decisions and foster a culture of connectivity and collaboration. By integrating SNA into your organizational practices, you can unlock the hidden potential of your informal networks, driving sustained success and growth.

Let the insights gained from this chapter inspire you to explore and leverage the informal networks within your organization. Embrace the tools and methods of SNA to create a more connected, innovative, and adaptive organization. As we continue to build on these concepts in the following chapters, you will be equipped with the knowledge and strategies to lead your organization through the complexities of modern business environments and achieve long-term success.

Part II: Advanced Concepts in Managing Change

Building on the foundational principles outlined in the first part of this book, Part II examines advanced concepts that are essential for managing change effectively within organizations. As the pace of change accelerates, organizations must adopt more sophisticated strategies to remain agile and resilient. This section explores a range of advanced topics, from whole systems change to the integration of mindfulness practices, each providing deeper insights into managing organizational transformation.

Chapter 6: Whole Systems Change

In this chapter, we introduce the concept of whole systems change, which involves a holistic approach to understanding and transforming organizations. We will delve into systems thinking, a methodology that enables leaders to see the organization as an interconnected web of relationships and processes. The chapter will cover techniques for mapping and understanding these systems, identifying leverage points where interventions can have the most significant impact. Through case studies, we will illustrate successful applications of whole systems change, highlighting the benefits and challenges of this comprehensive approach.

Chapter 7: Micro-Level Change: Team Dynamics and Process Improvements

Effective change management also requires attention to micro-level dynamics within teams and processes. This chapter focuses on enhancing team dynamics through strategies that promote effective communication and collaboration. We will explore how to leverage team strengths and recognize and reward team performance to foster a positive and productive work environment. Additionally, we will discuss process improvements that can streamline operations and support team efficiency, providing practical tools and techniques for driving micro-level change.

Chapter 8: Mindfulness and Stress Reduction

The health and well-being of employees are critical components of organizational success. Chapter 8 examines the impact of mindfulness on organizational health, presenting techniques for stress reduction that can enhance employee well-being and productivity. We will explore how to incorporate mindfulness into organizational practices, creating a culture that supports mental and emotional resilience. By integrating mindfulness, organizations can improve focus, reduce burnout, and foster a more supportive work environment.

Chapter 9: Knowledge Management

Knowledge is a strategic asset in any organization. This chapter discusses strategies for knowledge creation, sharing, and management, emphasizing the role of technology in facilitating these processes. We will explore how to build a knowledge-sharing culture that encourages continuous learning and innovation. Practical strategies for leveraging technology to manage knowledge more effectively will be presented, helping organizations to harness their collective expertise and drive competitive advantage.

Chapter 10: Collaborative Learning and Technology Strategy

In an increasingly digital world, integrating collaborative learning into organizational culture is vital. Chapter 10 focuses on aligning technology strategy with organizational goals to support collaborative learning. We will discuss various tools and platforms that facilitate learning and collaboration, ensuring that teams can work together seamlessly, regardless of physical location. This chapter provides insights into creating a technology strategy that enhances learning and collaboration, driving innovation and adaptability.

Part II of this book equips you with advanced strategies and concepts essential for managing change in today's complex and fast-paced business environment. By understanding and applying these advanced principles, you will be better prepared to lead your organization through transformational change, ensuring long-term success and sustainability.

Chapter 6: Whole Systems Change

In a world where change is constant and organizations must continuously adapt to survive and thrive, a holistic approach to transformation is essential. Chapter 6 introduces the concept of Whole Systems Change, a comprehensive method that considers the organization as an interconnected system. This approach moves beyond isolated interventions, focusing instead on understanding and addressing the complex web of relationships and interdependencies that characterize organizational life.

The Systems Thinking Approach is foundational to Whole Systems Change. Systems thinking involves viewing the organization as a whole, recognizing that changes in one area can have far-reaching impacts on other areas. This perspective allows leaders to see beyond linear cause-and-effect relationships, understanding instead how various elements within the organization interact dynamically. By adopting systems thinking, organizations can more effectively diagnose issues, identify opportunities, and implement changes that promote overall health and resilience.

Mapping and understanding organizational systems is a crucial step in this process. It involves creating visual representations of the organization's structures, processes, and relationships. These maps help reveal how different parts of the organization are connected, where bottlenecks or inefficiencies may exist, and how information and resources flow. This comprehensive understanding is essential for identifying areas that require attention and for developing targeted interventions that address root causes rather than symptoms.

Identifying leverage points for change is another key aspect of Whole Systems Change. Leverage points are strategic areas within the system where small changes can lead to significant improvements. By focusing efforts on these critical points, organizations can maximize the impact of their change initiatives. This requires a deep understanding of the system's dynamics and the ability to anticipate how changes will ripple through the organization.

Case studies of Whole Systems Change provide practical insights into how this approach can be applied effectively. These real-world examples illustrate the challenges and successes of organizations that have implemented whole systems change, offering valuable lessons and strategies that can be adapted to different contexts. By studying these cases, leaders can gain inspiration and practical guidance on how to navigate their own complex change initiatives.

In this chapter, you will learn about the principles and practices of Whole Systems Change. We will explore how systems thinking can transform your approach to organizational development, how to map and understand your organizational systems, and how to identify and act on leverage points for maximum impact. Through case studies, you will see how these concepts come to life in real organizational settings, providing a roadmap for implementing Whole Systems Change in your own organization. Embrace this holistic approach to drive meaningful and sustainable transformation, ensuring your organization is resilient, adaptable, and prepared for the future.

The Systems Thinking Approach is a holistic way of understanding and managing organizations by viewing them as complex, interconnected systems. Unlike traditional linear thinking, which focuses on cause-and-effect relationships, systems thinking emphasizes the interactions and interdependencies among various components within the organization. This approach helps leaders see the bigger picture and understand how changes in one part of the system can impact other parts, often in unexpected ways.

At its core, systems thinking involves recognizing patterns and structures that underlie organizational behavior. It encourages looking beyond immediate problems to identify underlying issues and root causes. By doing so, it provides a deeper understanding of how organizational processes, people, and resources interact. This perspective is crucial for diagnosing complex problems, designing effective interventions, and fostering a culture of continuous improvement.

One of the key principles of systems thinking is feedback loops. These loops can be reinforcing, where an action produces a result that influences more of the same action, leading to exponential growth or decline, or balancing, where an action produces a result that counteracts the initial action, promoting stability. Understanding these feedback loops helps organizations anticipate and manage dynamic behavior within the system.

Causal loop diagrams are a common tool used in systems thinking to visualize and analyze the relationships between different elements in the system. These diagrams map out how various factors influence each other, highlighting feedback loops and potential points of intervention. They provide a clear and comprehensive way to communicate complex systems dynamics, making it easier to identify leverage points for change.

Systems thinking also involves a shift from blame to learning. Instead of focusing on individual failures, it encourages looking at the system's design and operation to understand how it contributes to undesirable outcomes. This approach fosters a culture of learning and innovation, where employees are motivated to improve processes and systems continuously.

Adopting a systems thinking approach can lead to more sustainable and effective organizational change. By understanding the interconnectedness of various elements, leaders can design interventions that address root causes, align with organizational goals, and create lasting improvements. This approach also promotes resilience, as organizations become better equipped to adapt to changes and disruptions in their environment.

In practice, systems thinking requires collaboration and open communication across all levels of the organization. It involves engaging employees in the process of identifying issues and developing solutions, ensuring that diverse perspectives are considered. This inclusive approach not only leads to more robust solutions but also builds a shared understanding and commitment to organizational goals.

Overall, the Systems Thinking Approach offers a powerful framework for managing complex organizational challenges. By viewing the organization as a dynamic system and understanding the interplay of its components, leaders can drive meaningful and sustainable change, fostering a more adaptable and resilient organization.

Mapping and understanding organizational systems involve creating visual representations of the structures, processes, and relationships within an organization. This practice provides a comprehensive view of how different parts of the organization are interconnected and how they influence one another. By mapping these systems, organizations can identify bottlenecks, inefficiencies, and areas that require improvement.

The process begins with gathering detailed information about the organization's various components, including its departments, teams, workflows, and communication channels. This information is then used to create diagrams that illustrate the organization's structure and dynamics. These visual maps often take the form of flowcharts, network diagrams, or causal loop diagrams, each serving to highlight different aspects of the system.

Flowcharts are useful for mapping out processes step-by-step, showing how tasks are sequenced and how information or materials flow through the organization. They help identify redundancies, delays, and potential points of failure in processes. Network diagrams, on the other hand, focus on the relationships between individuals or groups within the organization. They illustrate how communication and collaboration occur, revealing key influencers, isolated individuals, and the overall connectivity of the organization.

Causal loop diagrams are particularly valuable in systems thinking as they depict the feedback loops that drive organizational behavior. These diagrams show how different variables affect each other, highlighting reinforcing loops that can lead to exponential growth or decline and balancing loops that stabilize the system. By understanding these feedback mechanisms, organizations can anticipate the long-term effects of changes and identify leverage points for effective interventions.

Mapping organizational systems also involves identifying key metrics and indicators that reflect the health and performance of the system. These metrics can include process efficiency, communication effectiveness, employee engagement, and customer satisfaction. By tracking these indicators, organizations can monitor the impact of changes and continuously refine their strategies for improvement.

In addition to creating visual maps, understanding organizational systems requires engaging with employees at all levels to gather insights and feedback. This collaborative approach ensures that the maps accurately reflect the reality of the organization and that any proposed changes are practical and supported by those who will implement them. Engaging employees in the mapping process also fosters a sense of ownership and commitment to the organization's goals.

Through mapping and understanding organizational systems, leaders can gain a holistic view of their organization, uncover hidden dynamics, and make informed decisions that drive sustainable improvement. This practice enables organizations to move beyond reactive problem-solving to proactive system design, creating a more resilient and adaptive organization. By continually refining their understanding of organizational systems, leaders can ensure that their strategies are aligned with the complex realities of their organization, ultimately leading to greater efficiency, innovation, and success.

Identifying leverage points for change is a crucial step in the process of transforming an organization. Leverage points are specific areas within a system where small shifts can lead to significant improvements. By focusing on these strategic points, organizations can maximize the impact of their change initiatives and achieve more sustainable results.

To identify leverage points, it is essential first to understand the underlying dynamics of the organizational system. This involves analyzing the interactions and feedback loops that drive behavior within the organization. Tools such as causal loop diagrams and system maps can help visualize these dynamics, highlighting areas where interventions might be most effective.

One common approach to finding leverage points is to look for bottlenecks or constraints that impede performance. These could be processes that consistently cause delays, areas where resources are insufficient, or points where communication breaks down. Addressing these constraints can often lead to substantial improvements in overall efficiency and effectiveness.

Another method is to identify key influencers within the organization. These are individuals or groups who have a significant impact on the behavior and attitudes of others. By engaging these influencers in the change process, organizations can more effectively promote new behaviors and practices across the system.

Feedback loops, both reinforcing and balancing, are also critical areas to examine when identifying leverage points. Reinforcing loops can lead to exponential growth or decline, depending on whether the feedback is positive or negative. Intervening in these loops can amplify desired changes or mitigate negative trends. Balancing loops, on the other hand, work to stabilize the system. Understanding how to strengthen or adjust these loops can help maintain equilibrium while still promoting change.

Cultural elements of the organization, such as shared values, norms, and beliefs, can serve as powerful leverage points.

Aligning change initiatives with the organization's culture can enhance acceptance and reduce resistance. For instance, if a company values innovation, leveraging this cultural aspect by encouraging and rewarding innovative ideas can accelerate the adoption of new processes or technologies.

Leverage points can also be found in organizational policies and procedures. Reviewing and revising outdated or ineffective policies can remove barriers to change and create a more supportive environment for new initiatives. This might involve simplifying approval processes, updating performance metrics, or introducing new incentives aligned with the desired changes.

It is important to remember that identifying and acting on leverage points requires continuous monitoring and adjustment. As changes are implemented, the dynamics of the system will evolve, potentially revealing new leverage points or shifting the effectiveness of existing ones. Regularly revisiting the system map and feedback loops ensures that the organization remains responsive and adaptive to ongoing changes.

By focusing on leverage points, organizations can drive significant improvements with targeted, strategic interventions. This approach not only enhances the efficiency and impact of change initiatives but also fosters a more dynamic and resilient organization. By continuously seeking out and leveraging these strategic points, leaders can steer their organizations through complex transformations and achieve sustained success.

Case studies of whole systems change provide valuable insights into how organizations can effectively implement comprehensive transformations by considering the entire organizational system. These examples illustrate the challenges and successes of adopting a holistic approach to change and offer practical lessons that can be applied in various contexts.

One notable case is that of General Electric (GE) during Jack Welch's tenure as CEO. Welch initiated a transformation program known as "Work-Out" to create a more flexible and efficient organization. The program aimed to eliminate unnecessary bureaucracy, empower employees, and improve overall performance. By involving employees at all levels in the decision-making process and focusing on the entire system rather than isolated departments, GE was able to streamline operations, reduce costs, and foster a culture of continuous improvement.

Another example is Toyota's adoption of the Toyota Production System (TPS), which revolutionized manufacturing practices worldwide. TPS is a comprehensive approach that integrates various elements such as just-in-time production, continuous improvement (Kaizen), and respect for people. By viewing the production process as a whole system, Toyota was able to eliminate waste, enhance efficiency, and improve product quality. This holistic approach allowed Toyota to become a global leader in the automotive industry and set new standards for manufacturing excellence.

The transformation of the healthcare system in Denmark provides a compelling case of whole systems change in the public sector. Faced with rising costs and an aging population, Denmark embarked on a series of reforms to improve the efficiency and quality of healthcare services. This involved restructuring hospitals, integrating primary and secondary care, and implementing new technologies to support patient-centered care. By taking a systems perspective, Denmark was able to create a more coordinated and efficient healthcare system that better meets the needs of its citizens.

Walmart's sustainability initiative is another example of whole systems change. Recognizing the impact of its operations on the environment, Walmart set ambitious goals to reduce waste, increase energy efficiency, and promote sustainable sourcing. This required changes across the entire supply chain, from suppliers to stores to consumers. By adopting a holistic approach and engaging stakeholders at all levels, Walmart was able to make significant progress toward its sustainability goals and set a new standard for corporate responsibility in the retail industry.

A final example is the transformation of the UK Ministry of Defence's procurement process. Faced with budget constraints and the need for greater efficiency, the Ministry undertook a comprehensive review of its procurement practices. By mapping the entire procurement system, identifying key leverage points, and involving stakeholders in the redesign process, the Ministry was able to streamline operations, reduce costs, and improve the delivery of critical defense capabilities.

These case studies demonstrate that whole systems change is a powerful approach to organizational transformation. By considering the entire system, organizations can address root causes of issues, align efforts across different parts of the organization, and achieve more sustainable and impactful results. Whether in the private or public sector, adopting a holistic perspective allows leaders to navigate complex challenges and drive meaningful change that benefits the entire organization.

In Chapter 6, we have explored the concept of Whole Systems Change, emphasizing the importance of viewing organizations as interconnected systems where changes in one area can significantly impact others. By adopting a Systems Thinking Approach, organizations can better understand the complex dynamics at play and design more effective and sustainable interventions.

We began by discussing the Systems Thinking Approach, which provides a holistic view of the organization, highlighting the importance of feedback loops and the interdependencies among various components. This approach helps leaders see beyond immediate problems to identify underlying issues and root causes, fostering a culture of continuous improvement and learning.

Mapping and understanding organizational systems is a crucial step in this process. Creating visual representations of the organization's structures, processes, and relationships allows for a comprehensive understanding of how different parts of the organization are connected and influence one another. This understanding is essential for identifying bottlenecks, inefficiencies, and areas that require improvement.

Identifying leverage points for change involves pinpointing specific areas within the system where small shifts can lead to significant improvements. By focusing on these strategic points, organizations can maximize the impact of their change initiatives and achieve more sustainable results. This requires a deep understanding of the system's dynamics and the ability to anticipate how changes will ripple through the organization.

Through case studies of Whole Systems Change, we have seen practical examples of how organizations like General Electric, Toyota, Denmark's healthcare system, Walmart, and the UK Ministry of Defence have successfully implemented comprehensive transformations. These examples illustrate the challenges and successes of adopting a holistic approach to change and offer valuable lessons and strategies that can be adapted to different contexts.

As we conclude this chapter, it is essential to recognize that Whole Systems Change is not a one-time effort but an ongoing process that requires continuous monitoring and adjustment. By embracing systems thinking, mapping and understanding organizational systems, identifying leverage points, and learning from real-world examples, leaders can drive meaningful and sustainable transformation in their organizations.

Moving forward, let the insights and strategies discussed in this chapter inspire you to adopt a holistic approach to change. Embrace the principles of Whole Systems Change to create a more resilient, adaptable, and high-performing organization. By doing so, you can navigate the complexities of modern business environments and achieve long-term success and growth. Through dedication and a proactive approach to understanding and managing the interconnectedness of your organization, you can lead your team toward a thriving future.

Chapter 7: Micro-Level Change: Team Dynamics and Process Improvements

While whole systems change offers a broad, strategic perspective on organizational transformation, micro-level change focuses on the intricacies of team dynamics and process improvements that drive day-to-day operations. In Chapter 7, we delve into the essential elements of micro-level change, emphasizing how enhancing team dynamics and refining processes can lead to significant improvements in performance and productivity.

Teams are the building blocks of any organization. The effectiveness of these teams depends on their dynamics, which encompass the interactions, relationships, and behaviors among team members. Enhancing team dynamics involves fostering an environment where trust, respect, and open communication thrive. By doing so, organizations can build cohesive teams capable of collaborating effectively and achieving their goals.

Effective communication and collaboration are crucial for the success of any team. Clear, open, and honest communication ensures that team members are aligned, informed, and able to work together efficiently. Collaboration, on the other hand, involves leveraging the diverse skills and perspectives of team members to solve problems and innovate. In this chapter, we will explore strategies to improve both communication and collaboration within teams, ensuring that everyone is working towards common objectives.

Leveraging team strengths is another critical aspect of micro-level change. Every team comprises individuals with unique skills, experiences, and strengths. Identifying and harnessing these strengths can enhance team performance and job satisfaction. This chapter will discuss methods for recognizing individual strengths and assigning roles and tasks that align with these abilities, thereby maximizing the potential of each team member.

Recognizing and rewarding team performance is essential for maintaining motivation and engagement. Regular recognition of both individual and team achievements fosters a culture of appreciation and encourages continuous improvement. By implementing effective reward systems, organizations can reinforce desired behaviors and outcomes, driving higher levels of performance and commitment.

In this chapter, you will learn practical strategies for enhancing team dynamics, improving communication and collaboration, leveraging team strengths, and recognizing and rewarding performance. These micro-level changes, while often subtle, can have a profound impact on overall organizational success. By focusing on the details of how teams operate and continuously refining processes, leaders can create a more dynamic, responsive, and high-performing organization.

As we explore these concepts, remember that the small changes you make at the team level can ripple outward, influencing the broader organization. By investing in your teams and processes, you can drive significant improvements in efficiency, innovation, and employee satisfaction, ultimately contributing to the long-term success of your organization.

Enhancing team dynamics is essential for fostering a collaborative and high-performing work environment. Effective team dynamics are built on a foundation of trust, respect, and open communication among team members. Establishing this foundation begins with creating an atmosphere where individuals feel safe to express their ideas, concerns, and feedback without fear of judgment or retribution. This psychological safety encourages participation and innovation, as team members are more likely to share creative solutions and engage in productive discussions.

Understanding the different roles and personalities within the team is crucial for enhancing dynamics. Each team member brings unique strengths, skills, and perspectives to the table. By recognizing and valuing these differences, leaders can ensure that tasks and responsibilities are aligned with individual capabilities, promoting a sense of purpose and satisfaction. Encouraging team members to appreciate and leverage each other's strengths fosters a more cohesive and supportive team environment.

Effective communication is at the heart of strong team dynamics. Clear and consistent communication helps prevent misunderstandings and ensures that everyone is on the same page. This involves not only sharing information but also actively listening to others. Regular team meetings, check-ins, and open forums for discussion can facilitate better communication and collaboration. Additionally, using collaborative tools and technologies can help streamline communication, especially in remote or distributed teams.

Conflict is a natural part of any team dynamic, but how it is managed can significantly impact the team's effectiveness. Constructive conflict resolution involves addressing issues promptly and fairly, focusing on finding solutions rather than assigning blame. Encouraging open dialogue and providing training in conflict resolution skills can help team members navigate disagreements in a healthy and productive manner.

Building trust among team members is another critical component of enhancing team dynamics. Trust is developed through reliability, transparency, and mutual respect. Leaders can model trust-building behaviors by being consistent, honest, and fair in their interactions. Trust is also strengthened when team members deliver on their commitments and support each other in achieving common goals.

Creating opportunities for team bonding and social interaction can further enhance team dynamics. Team-building activities, whether formal exercises or informal gatherings, help build relationships and foster a sense of camaraderie. These activities can break down barriers, improve morale, and create a more positive team culture.

Feedback and continuous improvement are integral to enhancing team dynamics. Regularly soliciting and providing feedback helps identify areas for improvement and reinforces positive behaviors. Implementing a continuous improvement mindset encourages teams to reflect on their performance, learn from their experiences, and make necessary adjustments to enhance their effectiveness.

Enhancing team dynamics involves fostering a culture of trust, respect, and open communication. Understanding and leveraging individual strengths, managing conflict constructively, building trust, promoting team bonding, and encouraging continuous improvement are all essential elements. By focusing on these areas, leaders can create a supportive and collaborative environment where teams can thrive and achieve their full potential. Strong team dynamics not only improve individual and collective performance but also contribute to a more positive and resilient organizational culture.

Effective communication and collaboration are critical components of successful team dynamics and overall organizational performance. Communication involves the clear and concise exchange of information, ideas, and feedback among team members. It ensures that everyone is aligned, informed, and working towards common objectives. Collaboration, on the other hand, is the process of working together towards a shared goal, leveraging the diverse skills and perspectives of each team member to achieve the best possible outcomes.

Creating an environment that supports open and honest communication is essential. This begins with fostering a culture where team members feel comfortable sharing their thoughts and opinions without fear of judgment or retribution. Leaders play a crucial role in modeling transparent communication by being open about goals, challenges, and expectations. Regular team meetings, both formal and informal, provide opportunities for team members to discuss progress, address issues, and share ideas.

Active listening is a vital aspect of effective communication. It involves not only hearing what others are saying but also understanding and considering their perspectives. This requires team members to be fully present during conversations, refrain from interrupting, and ask clarifying questions when needed. Active listening helps build trust and ensures that all voices are heard and valued.

Using the right communication tools and technologies can enhance both communication and collaboration, especially in remote or distributed teams. Tools like video conferencing, instant messaging, and project management software facilitate real-time communication and help keep everyone connected and engaged. These tools also allow for the sharing of documents, tracking of tasks, and coordination of activities, making it easier for teams to collaborate effectively.

Setting clear expectations and goals is another important aspect of effective communication and collaboration. When team members understand their roles and responsibilities, as well as the objectives they are working towards, they can coordinate their efforts more efficiently. This clarity helps prevent misunderstandings and ensures that everyone is moving in the same direction.

Collaboration thrives in an environment where team members are encouraged to share their expertise and contribute to problem-solving. This involves creating opportunities for cross-functional teamwork, where individuals from different departments or areas of expertise come together to work on projects. Such collaboration can lead to more innovative solutions and a more integrated approach to achieving organizational goals.

Building strong interpersonal relationships within the team also enhances communication and collaboration. When team members trust and respect one another, they are more likely to engage in open dialogue and work together effectively. Team-building activities and social interactions can help strengthen these relationships, fostering a sense of camaraderie and mutual support.

Feedback is a crucial component of both communication and collaboration. Regularly providing and soliciting feedback helps team members understand their strengths and areas for improvement, promotes continuous learning, and encourages a culture of accountability. Constructive feedback should be specific, actionable, and delivered in a supportive manner, focusing on behaviors and outcomes rather than personal attributes.

Effective communication and collaboration are foundational to high-performing teams and successful organizations. By fostering an environment of open and honest communication, practicing active listening, utilizing appropriate tools and technologies, setting clear expectations, encouraging cross-functional teamwork, building strong relationships, and promoting continuous feedback, leaders can create a collaborative culture that drives innovation, efficiency, and overall success.

Leveraging team strengths involves recognizing and utilizing the unique skills, talents, and perspectives that each team member brings to the table. This approach not only enhances team performance but also boosts individual job satisfaction and engagement. The process begins with identifying the strengths of each team member through assessments, feedback, and observation. Understanding what each person excels at allows leaders to assign roles and tasks that align with their abilities, thereby maximizing efficiency and productivity.

Effective leaders foster an environment where these strengths can be utilized to their fullest potential. This involves creating opportunities for team members to apply their skills in meaningful ways and encouraging them to take ownership of their tasks. By aligning responsibilities with individual strengths, leaders can ensure that each team member is working in a role that suits them best, which leads to higher motivation and better results.

Collaboration is a key aspect of leveraging team strengths. When team members understand and appreciate each other's strengths, they can work together more effectively, complementing each other's abilities and covering for each other's weaknesses. This collaborative approach not only improves performance but also fosters a sense of unity and mutual respect within the team.

Developing a culture of continuous learning and development is essential for leveraging team strengths. Encouraging team members to pursue professional development opportunities, such as training programs, workshops, and certifications, helps them build on their existing strengths and acquire new skills. Leaders should provide support and resources for ongoing learning, helping team members stay current with industry trends and advancements.

Recognizing and celebrating the strengths and contributions of team members is crucial for maintaining high morale and motivation. Acknowledging individual achievements and providing positive reinforcement can boost confidence and encourage further excellence. Public recognition, rewards, and personalized feedback are effective ways to show appreciation and highlight the value of each team member's strengths.

Leaders should also encourage a growth mindset within the team, promoting the belief that abilities and talents can be developed through dedication and hard work. This mindset helps team members view challenges as opportunities to grow rather than obstacles to avoid. By fostering a culture that values learning and improvement, leaders can help team members continuously enhance their strengths and contribute more effectively to the team's success.

Flexibility in roles and responsibilities can also be beneficial. Allowing team members to take on different roles or projects that align with their strengths can lead to increased engagement and innovation. This approach not only utilizes their current skills but also helps them develop new ones, making the team more adaptable and versatile.

Effective communication is essential for leveraging team strengths. Leaders should regularly communicate the importance of each team member's contributions and how they align with the team's goals. This communication helps team members understand their role within the larger context and feel valued for their unique contributions.

Leveraging team strengths involves recognizing individual skills, aligning roles with those strengths, fostering collaboration, promoting continuous learning, and celebrating achievements. By creating an environment that values and utilizes each team member's strengths, leaders can enhance team performance, boost morale, and drive overall organizational success. This approach not only maximizes the potential of each individual but also contributes to a more dynamic, innovative, and resilient team.

Recognizing and rewarding team performance is crucial for maintaining high levels of motivation, engagement, and job satisfaction among team members. It involves acknowledging both individual and collective achievements in a meaningful way that reinforces positive behaviors and outcomes. Recognition can take many forms, from formal awards and public acknowledgment to personalized feedback and informal praise. The key is to ensure that recognition is timely, specific, and genuine, so that team members feel valued and appreciated for their contributions.

Creating a culture of recognition begins with leaders who consistently model and promote the importance of acknowledging hard work and success. By regularly highlighting achievements during meetings, in communications, and through organizational channels, leaders can set a standard that encourages others to do the same. This continuous recognition helps build a positive work environment where employees feel motivated to excel.

Effective recognition should be specific, detailing what the individual or team did well and how it contributed to the organization's goals. This specificity not only reinforces the behaviors that led to success but also provides a clear understanding of what is valued within the organization. For example, recognizing a team for completing a project ahead of schedule and under budget highlights the importance of efficiency and cost management.

Personalized recognition is also important. Understanding what type of recognition resonates most with each team member allows leaders to tailor their approach. Some employees may value public acknowledgment, while others might prefer private praise or tangible rewards. By taking the time to understand these preferences, leaders can ensure that their recognition efforts have the greatest impact.

Reward systems can complement recognition efforts by providing tangible incentives for high performance. These rewards can include bonuses, promotions, additional time off, or professional development opportunities. The key is to align rewards with the values and goals of the organization, ensuring they reinforce desired behaviors and outcomes. Effective reward systems are transparent and fair, with clear criteria for what constitutes exceptional performance.

Team-based rewards are particularly effective for fostering collaboration and collective effort. Recognizing and rewarding the achievements of an entire team emphasizes the importance of working together towards common goals. This approach helps build a sense of unity and shared purpose, encouraging team members to support one another and collaborate more effectively.

Regular feedback is another critical component of recognizing and rewarding performance. Providing constructive feedback helps employees understand their strengths and areas for improvement, fostering continuous development and growth. Feedback should be balanced, highlighting both achievements and opportunities for improvement, and delivered in a supportive and respectful manner.

In addition to formal recognition and rewards, informal gestures of appreciation can have a significant impact on team morale. Simple acts such as a handwritten thank-you note, a shout-out during a meeting, or a casual compliment can make employees feel appreciated and valued. These everyday gestures help create a positive and supportive work environment.

Leaders should continually seek opportunities to acknowledge and celebrate achievements, ensuring that recognition is an integral part of the organizational culture. By doing so, they can maintain high levels of motivation and engagement, drive continuous improvement, and foster a positive and dynamic work environment. Recognizing and rewarding team performance involves timely, specific, and personalized acknowledgment of both individual and collective achievements. By creating a culture of recognition, aligning rewards with organizational goals, providing regular feedback, and incorporating informal gestures of appreciation, leaders can enhance motivation, engagement, and job satisfaction. This approach not only boosts individual performance but also strengthens team cohesion and drives overall organizational success.

Chapter 7 has delved into the micro-level changes that are essential for enhancing team dynamics and process improvements within organizations. By focusing on the intricacies of team interactions and refining day-to-day operations, organizations can significantly boost their overall performance and create a more cohesive and productive work environment.

We began by discussing the importance of enhancing team dynamics, which involves fostering a culture of trust, respect, and open communication. Understanding and leveraging the unique strengths of each team member, managing conflicts constructively, and encouraging continuous feedback and improvement are all crucial components of strong team dynamics. By building these foundations, teams can operate more effectively and achieve their goals with greater efficiency and collaboration.

Effective communication and collaboration were highlighted as critical aspects of successful team performance. Clear and consistent communication ensures that everyone is aligned and informed, while active listening and the use of appropriate tools and technologies facilitate seamless collaboration. By setting clear expectations, encouraging cross-functional teamwork, and fostering strong interpersonal relationships, organizations can create an environment where communication and collaboration thrive.

Leveraging team strengths involves recognizing and utilizing the unique skills and talents of each team member. By aligning roles and responsibilities with individual strengths, promoting a growth mindset, and providing opportunities for continuous learning and development, leaders can maximize the potential of their teams. This approach not only enhances team performance but also boosts individual job satisfaction and engagement.

Recognizing and rewarding team performance is essential for maintaining high levels of motivation and commitment. Timely, specific, and genuine recognition, coupled with fair and transparent reward systems, reinforces positive behaviors and outcomes. By celebrating both individual and collective achievements, providing regular feedback, and incorporating informal gestures of appreciation, leaders can foster a positive and supportive work environment.

As we conclude this chapter, it is important to recognize that the small changes made at the team level can have a profound impact on the broader organization. By focusing on enhancing team dynamics, improving communication and collaboration, leveraging team strengths, and recognizing and rewarding performance, leaders can create a more dynamic, innovative, and resilient organization.

Moving forward, let the insights and strategies discussed in this chapter inspire you to invest in your teams and processes. By nurturing the micro-level changes that drive day-to-day operations, you can build a strong foundation for sustained success and growth. Through dedication, continuous improvement, and a commitment to fostering a positive team environment, you can lead your organization to achieve its strategic goals and thrive in an ever-changing business landscape.

Chapter 8: Mindfulness and Stress Reduction

In the fast-paced and often high-pressure world of modern business, maintaining organizational health and employee well-being is more crucial than ever. Chapter 8 explores the transformative power of mindfulness and stress reduction techniques in fostering a healthier, more resilient workforce. As organizations strive for high performance and continuous improvement, integrating mindfulness practices can significantly enhance employee engagement, reduce stress, and improve overall productivity.

Mindfulness, the practice of being fully present and engaged in the moment, has gained widespread recognition for its positive impact on mental and physical health. Within the context of an organization, mindfulness can lead to greater emotional intelligence, improved focus, and better decision-making. Employees who practice mindfulness are more likely to manage stress effectively, maintain a positive outlook, and engage in constructive communication. These benefits contribute to a more supportive and dynamic work environment, where individuals can thrive both personally and professionally.

Stress reduction is a critical component of organizational health. Chronic stress can lead to burnout, decreased productivity, and higher turnover rates. By implementing effective stress reduction techniques, organizations can create a more balanced and sustainable work culture. Techniques such as deep breathing exercises, meditation, and progressive muscle relaxation can help employees manage stress and enhance their overall well-being. Additionally, promoting a healthy work-life balance and providing resources for mental health support are essential strategies for reducing workplace stress.

Incorporating mindfulness into organizational practices involves integrating mindfulness techniques into daily routines and organizational policies. This can include offering mindfulness training programs, creating dedicated spaces for relaxation and meditation, and encouraging regular breaks for mindfulness exercises. Leaders play a vital role in modeling mindful behavior and fostering a culture that values well-being. By prioritizing mindfulness and stress reduction, organizations can enhance their resilience, foster a more positive work environment, and improve overall performance.

As we explore the impact of mindfulness on organizational health, techniques for stress reduction, and strategies for incorporating mindfulness into daily practices, you will gain practical insights and tools to create a healthier, more productive workplace. Embracing mindfulness and stress reduction is not only beneficial for individual employees but also contributes to the long-term success and sustainability of the organization. Through this chapter, you will learn how to implement these practices effectively, leading to a more engaged, focused, and resilient workforce.

Mindfulness has a profound impact on organizational health, influencing various aspects of employee well-being and overall productivity. At its core, mindfulness involves being fully present and aware in the moment, fostering a deeper connection with one's thoughts, emotions, and environment. This heightened awareness can lead to numerous benefits for both individuals and the organization as a whole.

Incorporating mindfulness into the workplace can significantly reduce stress levels among employees. Chronic stress is a common issue in modern organizations, leading to burnout, absenteeism, and decreased productivity. Mindfulness practices such as meditation and deep breathing exercises help individuals manage stress more effectively by promoting relaxation and reducing the physiological effects of stress on the body. Employees who regularly practice mindfulness are better equipped to handle challenging situations calmly and with greater resilience.

Being mindful also enhances emotional intelligence, which is crucial for effective communication and collaboration. Employees with high emotional intelligence can better understand and manage their emotions, leading to more constructive interactions with colleagues. This improved emotional regulation fosters a positive work environment, where conflicts are resolved more efficiently and relationships are strengthened. As a result, teamwork and overall morale improve, contributing to a more cohesive and supportive organizational culture. Another significant impact of mindfulness is the enhancement of focus and concentration. In a workplace filled with distractions, maintaining attention on tasks can be challenging. Mindfulness practices train the mind to stay present, improving an individual's ability to concentrate on the task at hand. This heightened focus leads to increased productivity and higher quality work, as employees are less likely to be sidetracked by external or internal distractions.

Mindfulness also supports better decision-making processes. By fostering a non-judgmental awareness of thoughts and emotions, mindfulness helps individuals approach problems with a clear and balanced mindset. This clarity allows for more rational and thoughtful decision-making, reducing the likelihood of impulsive or emotion-driven choices. Consequently, the organization benefits from more strategic and effective decisions at all levels. Furthermore, mindfulness promotes overall well-being, which is closely linked to job satisfaction and retention. Employees who feel mentally and physically healthy are more likely to be engaged and committed to their work. This engagement translates to higher levels of performance and a lower likelihood of turnover, as employees feel more satisfied with their roles and the organizational environment.

Leaders who practice and promote mindfulness can also set a powerful example for their teams. Mindful leadership involves being fully present in interactions, demonstrating empathy, and making thoughtful decisions. This leadership style fosters a culture of mindfulness within the organization, encouraging employees to adopt similar practices and attitudes. As a result, the entire organization can benefit from the collective improvements in well-being, communication, and performance.

Mindfulness has a significant and positive impact on organizational health. By reducing stress, enhancing emotional intelligence, improving focus and concentration, supporting better decision-making, and promoting overall well-being, mindfulness contributes to a more productive, resilient, and engaged workforce. Implementing mindfulness practices in the workplace can lead to a healthier and more harmonious organizational environment, driving long-term success and sustainability.

Stress reduction techniques are essential for maintaining a healthy and productive workforce. These techniques help employees manage stress effectively, promoting both mental and physical well-being. One of the most effective stress reduction techniques is mindfulness meditation. This practice involves focusing on the present moment, paying attention to thoughts, feelings, and sensations without judgment. Regular meditation can reduce stress by calming the mind and decreasing anxiety levels.

Deep breathing exercises are another simple yet powerful method for stress reduction. Controlled breathing helps activate the body's relaxation response, reducing heart rate and lowering blood pressure. Techniques such as diaphragmatic breathing, where one breathes deeply into the abdomen rather than shallowly into the chest, can be practiced anywhere and provide immediate stress relief.

Progressive muscle relaxation involves systematically tensing and then relaxing different muscle groups in the body. This technique helps individuals become more aware of physical tension and learn how to release it, promoting overall relaxation. Practicing progressive muscle relaxation regularly can reduce stress and improve sleep quality.

Physical activity is a well-known stress reliever. Exercise releases endorphins, which are natural mood lifters, and can also serve as a distraction from daily stressors. Activities such as walking, running, yoga, and strength training can help reduce stress levels and improve overall health.

Maintaining a healthy work-life balance is crucial for stress management. Encouraging employees to take regular breaks, use their vacation days, and establish boundaries between work and personal life can prevent burnout and promote long-term well-being. Flexible work arrangements, such as remote work or flexible hours, can also help employees manage their responsibilities more effectively.

Engaging in hobbies and leisure activities provides a break from work-related stress. Activities that individuals enjoy, whether it's reading, gardening, painting, or playing a musical instrument, can provide a sense of accomplishment and relaxation, reducing overall stress.

Social support is another important factor in stress reduction. Building strong relationships with colleagues, friends, and family provides a network of support that can help individuals cope with stress. Encouraging social interactions and team-building activities within the workplace can foster a supportive environment and reduce feelings of isolation.

Mindfulness practices can be integrated into the workplace through various initiatives. Offering mindfulness training programs, creating dedicated spaces for relaxation and meditation, and encouraging regular mindfulness exercises can help employees incorporate these practices into their daily routines. Additionally, providing resources such as apps or guided meditation sessions can make it easier for employees to access mindfulness practices.

Healthy eating and adequate sleep are also vital for stress management. A balanced diet provides the necessary nutrients for the body to function optimally, while sufficient sleep helps regulate mood and cognitive function. Employers can support healthy habits by offering nutritious food options at work and promoting the importance of sleep hygiene.

Time management techniques can help employees manage their workload more effectively, reducing stress. Prioritizing tasks, setting realistic goals, and breaking projects into smaller, manageable steps can prevent feelings of overwhelm. Encouraging employees to focus on one task at a time and take regular breaks can also improve productivity and reduce stress.

Incorporating stress reduction techniques into daily life can lead to significant improvements in overall well-being. By practicing mindfulness meditation, deep breathing exercises, progressive muscle relaxation, physical activity, maintaining a work-life balance, engaging in hobbies, seeking social support, adopting healthy habits, and managing time effectively, individuals can better manage stress and enhance their quality of life. Organizations that support these practices create a healthier, more resilient workforce, contributing to long-term success and sustainability.

Incorporating mindfulness into organizational practices involves integrating mindfulness techniques into the daily routines and culture of the workplace. This process begins with leadership commitment, where leaders model mindfulness behaviors and prioritize the well-being of their employees. By demonstrating a genuine commitment to mindfulness, leaders can set the tone for the entire organization.

Organizations can start by offering mindfulness training programs that teach employees the basics of mindfulness meditation, breathing exercises, and other stress-reduction techniques. These programs can be conducted through workshops, online courses, or guided sessions led by experienced practitioners. Providing access to these resources helps employees develop the skills needed to practice mindfulness effectively.

Creating dedicated spaces for relaxation and meditation within the workplace can further support mindfulness practices. These spaces should be quiet, comfortable, and free from distractions, allowing employees to take a few moments to reset and recharge during their workday. Encouraging regular breaks for mindfulness exercises can help employees maintain focus and manage stress more effectively.

Incorporating mindfulness into meetings and daily routines is another effective strategy. Starting meetings with a brief mindfulness exercise, such as deep breathing or a short meditation, can help participants center themselves and improve their attention and engagement. Additionally, promoting mindful communication practices, such as active listening and being fully present during conversations, can enhance collaboration and reduce misunderstandings.

Organizations can also provide resources and tools to support mindfulness practices. This might include subscriptions to mindfulness apps, access to guided meditation recordings, or offering books and articles on mindfulness techniques. Making these resources readily available encourages employees to integrate mindfulness into their daily lives.

Flexible work arrangements, such as remote work options or flexible hours, can support mindfulness by allowing employees to create a work environment that suits their needs. Flexibility helps employees manage their responsibilities more effectively, reducing stress and promoting a healthier work-life balance.

Recognizing and rewarding employees who embrace mindfulness practices can further embed these practices into the organizational culture. Publicly acknowledging the efforts of employees who participate in mindfulness programs or demonstrate mindful behaviors reinforces the importance of these practices and encourages others to follow suit.

Promoting a culture of openness and acceptance around mindfulness is crucial. Encouraging employees to share their experiences with mindfulness and how it has benefited them can create a supportive community. This openness helps destigmatize the practice and makes it more accessible to everyone within the organization.

Regularly evaluating the impact of mindfulness initiatives on employee well-being and organizational performance can help refine these practices. Collecting feedback through surveys or informal check-ins allows organizations to understand what works well and where improvements can be made. This continuous improvement approach ensures that mindfulness practices remain relevant and effective.

Incorporating mindfulness into organizational practices is a holistic approach that involves leadership commitment, providing training and resources, creating supportive environments, integrating mindfulness into daily routines, offering flexible work arrangements, recognizing and rewarding participation, promoting openness, and continuously evaluating impact. By embedding mindfulness into the fabric of the organization, leaders can foster a healthier, more resilient, and productive workforce, contributing to the long-term success and well-being of the organization.

In Chapter 8, we have explored the transformative power of mindfulness and stress reduction techniques in enhancing organizational health and employee well-being. By incorporating mindfulness into daily routines and organizational practices, companies can create a more resilient, focused, and productive workforce.

We began by discussing the impact of mindfulness on organizational health. Mindfulness, through practices like meditation and deep breathing, reduces stress and promotes mental clarity, leading to improved focus, emotional intelligence, and decision-making. These benefits extend to better communication, stronger team dynamics, and overall higher morale and job satisfaction. Employees who practice mindfulness are better equipped to handle stress and maintain a positive outlook, contributing to a healthier organizational culture.

Effective stress reduction techniques are essential for maintaining a balanced and sustainable work environment. Practices such as mindfulness meditation, deep breathing exercises, progressive muscle relaxation, physical activity, and maintaining a healthy work-life balance help individuals manage stress effectively. By promoting these techniques, organizations can prevent burnout, enhance productivity, and improve overall employee well-being.

Incorporating mindfulness into organizational practices involves integrating these techniques into the workplace culture. Leadership commitment to modeling mindfulness behaviors and prioritizing employee well-being is crucial. Offering mindfulness training programs, creating dedicated spaces for relaxation, and encouraging regular breaks for mindfulness exercises can help employees integrate these practices into their daily routines. Additionally, promoting mindful communication and providing resources such as mindfulness apps and guided meditations support ongoing practice.

Flexible work arrangements, recognizing and rewarding mindfulness practices, and fostering a culture of openness and acceptance around mindfulness further embed these practices into the organization. Continuous evaluation and refinement of mindfulness initiatives ensure that they remain effective and relevant.

By embracing mindfulness and stress reduction, organizations can build a more positive and dynamic work environment. These practices not only benefit individual employees but also contribute to the overall success and sustainability of the organization. The insights and strategies discussed in this chapter offer practical tools for creating a workplace where mindfulness and well-being are integral to daily operations.

As we conclude Chapter 8, let the principles of mindfulness inspire you to prioritize well-being and resilience in your organization. By integrating mindfulness and stress reduction techniques, you can enhance employee engagement, improve performance, and foster a healthier, more supportive workplace culture. These efforts will lead to long-term benefits for both individuals and the organization, driving sustained success and growth.

Moving forward, apply the knowledge and practices from this chapter to create a mindful and resilient organization. Through dedication to mindfulness and stress reduction, you can lead your team toward greater well-being and productivity, ensuring that your organization thrives in the face of challenges and opportunities.

Chapter 9: Knowledge Management

In today's rapidly evolving business environment, knowledge is one of the most valuable assets an organization can possess. Effective knowledge management is essential for fostering innovation, improving decision-making, and maintaining a competitive edge. Chapter 9 delves into the critical role of knowledge management in organizational success, exploring strategies for creating, sharing, and managing knowledge, the impact of technology on knowledge processes, and the importance of building a culture that values knowledge sharing and continuous learning.

Knowledge management encompasses the systematic approach to capturing, organizing, sharing, and analyzing an organization's knowledge assets. These assets include both explicit knowledge, such as documented processes and procedures, and tacit knowledge, which resides in the experiences and insights of employees. By effectively managing these knowledge assets, organizations can ensure that valuable information is accessible and usable, driving efficiency and innovation.

Strategies for knowledge creation, sharing, and management are foundational to effective knowledge management. Knowledge creation involves fostering an environment where new ideas and insights can emerge through collaboration and innovation. Sharing knowledge ensures that this valuable information is disseminated throughout the organization, breaking down silos and promoting a culture of transparency. Effective management of knowledge involves organizing and storing information in a way that makes it easily retrievable and usable, enhancing decision-making and problem-solving capabilities.

Technology plays a pivotal role in knowledge management. Advanced tools and platforms facilitate the capture, storage, and dissemination of knowledge, making it easier for employees to access the information they need. From document management systems and intranets to collaboration tools and artificial intelligence, technology enhances the efficiency and effectiveness of knowledge management processes. By leveraging these technological solutions, organizations can streamline their knowledge workflows and ensure that valuable insights are not lost.

Building a knowledge-sharing culture is essential for sustaining effective knowledge management. This involves creating an environment where employees are encouraged and rewarded for sharing their expertise and insights. Leaders play a crucial role in modeling and promoting knowledge-sharing behaviors, fostering trust, and breaking down barriers to collaboration. By cultivating a culture that values continuous learning and knowledge exchange, organizations can enhance their collective intelligence and drive ongoing improvement.

Inviting team members to be change agents and lifelong learners is a powerful strategy for embedding knowledge management into the organizational fabric. Encouraging employees to take ownership of their learning and development not only enhances their individual capabilities but also contributes to the organization's overall knowledge base. Providing opportunities for professional growth, such as training programs, mentorship, and access to learning resources, empowers employees to continuously expand their skills and share their knowledge with others.

As we explore the strategies for knowledge creation, sharing, and management, the role of technology, and the importance of building a knowledge-sharing culture, you will gain practical insights into how to implement effective knowledge management practices in your organization. Embracing these principles will help you create a more informed, innovative, and adaptive organization, capable of thriving in an ever-changing business landscape.

Let this chapter guide you in developing a comprehensive knowledge management strategy that leverages technology, fosters a culture of learning, and empowers your team members to be proactive agents of change. By doing so, you can ensure that your organization remains at the forefront of innovation and excellence, continually evolving and growing in the face of new challenges and opportunities.

Knowledge creation involves fostering an environment where new ideas and insights can emerge through collaboration and innovation. This process requires encouraging creativity and experimentation, allowing employees to explore new approaches and solutions. Organizations can support knowledge creation by providing resources for research and development, setting aside time for brainstorming sessions, and creating cross-functional teams to tackle complex problems from multiple perspectives.

Sharing knowledge ensures that valuable information is disseminated throughout the organization, breaking down silos and promoting a culture of transparency. Effective knowledge sharing can be achieved through regular meetings, workshops, and training sessions where employees can present their findings and share their expertise. Creating a centralized repository for knowledge, such as an intranet or a knowledge management system, allows employees to access and contribute information easily. Encouraging open communication and collaboration through digital platforms and social networks also facilitates the exchange of ideas and best practices.

Managing knowledge involves organizing and storing information in a way that makes it easily retrievable and usable, enhancing decision-making and problem-solving capabilities. Implementing a robust document management system helps categorize and archive documents, making it simple for employees to find relevant information when needed. Regularly updating and maintaining the knowledge base ensures that it remains accurate and current. Additionally, establishing clear protocols for data governance and security protects sensitive information and ensures compliance with regulatory requirements.

Incentivizing knowledge sharing and management is crucial for sustaining these practices. Recognizing and rewarding employees who actively contribute to the knowledge base and share their expertise can motivate others to do the same. Creating formal recognition programs or integrating knowledge-sharing behaviors into performance evaluations reinforces the importance of these activities.

Leadership plays a pivotal role in driving knowledge management initiatives. Leaders must model knowledge-sharing behaviors, demonstrate the value of collective intelligence, and create an environment where continuous learning is prioritized. By fostering a culture that values knowledge creation, sharing, and management, leaders can ensure that these practices become ingrained in the organizational fabric.

Regularly assessing and refining knowledge management strategies is essential for continuous improvement. Collecting feedback from employees, analyzing the effectiveness of knowledge-sharing activities, and staying updated on new tools and technologies can help organizations adapt their approaches to meet evolving needs. This ongoing evaluation ensures that knowledge management remains a dynamic and integral part of the organization's operations.

Effective knowledge creation, sharing, and management require a strategic and holistic approach. By fostering an environment that encourages innovation, facilitating open communication and collaboration, organizing information efficiently, incentivizing participation, and providing strong leadership, organizations can harness the full potential of their knowledge assets. This approach not only enhances individual and collective performance but also drives organizational growth and success in an increasingly competitive and fast-paced business landscape.

Technology plays a crucial role in knowledge management by providing the tools and platforms necessary to capture, store, and disseminate information effectively. Advanced technologies facilitate the seamless integration of knowledge management processes into daily operations, making it easier for employees to access and share valuable information. Document management systems help organize and archive documents, ensuring that knowledge is stored systematically and can be retrieved quickly when needed. These systems support the categorization and tagging of documents, enabling efficient searches and reducing the time spent looking for information.

Collaboration tools such as intranets, wikis, and cloud-based platforms enhance knowledge sharing by creating centralized repositories where employees can contribute and access information. These platforms support real-time collaboration, allowing team members to work together regardless of their physical location. Features like version control and collaborative editing ensure that the most current and accurate information is available to all users.

Artificial intelligence (AI) and machine learning (ML) technologies further enhance knowledge management by automating the organization and retrieval of information. AI-powered search engines can analyze user queries to provide more relevant results, while ML algorithms can identify patterns and trends in data, helping organizations gain insights and make informed decisions. Chatbots and virtual assistants can also facilitate knowledge access by answering common questions and guiding users to the appropriate resources.

Data analytics tools play a significant role in knowledge management by analyzing large volumes of data to extract meaningful insights. These tools help organizations understand how knowledge is being used, identify gaps in the knowledge base, and measure the impact of knowledge management initiatives. Analytics can also track user behavior and preferences, allowing for the personalization of content and recommendations.

Social media and enterprise social networks foster informal knowledge sharing and collaboration among employees. These platforms enable the exchange of ideas, experiences, and best practices in a more casual and interactive manner. They also help build a sense of community and encourage engagement, which can enhance overall knowledge sharing within the organization.

Mobile technology extends the reach of knowledge management by providing access to information on the go. Mobile apps and responsive web designs ensure that employees can access the knowledge base from their smartphones and tablets, increasing flexibility and convenience. This is particularly beneficial for remote workers and those who frequently travel, ensuring that they remain connected and informed.

Security technologies are essential for protecting sensitive information and ensuring compliance with regulatory requirements. Encryption, access controls, and secure authentication methods safeguard the knowledge base against unauthorized access and data breaches. Regular security audits and updates help maintain the integrity and confidentiality of organizational knowledge.

The role of technology in knowledge management is multifaceted, encompassing the organization, sharing, and protection of information. By leveraging advanced tools and platforms, organizations can streamline knowledge management processes, enhance collaboration, and gain valuable insights. Effective use of technology ensures that knowledge is readily accessible, secure, and used to its fullest potential, driving innovation and supporting strategic objectives.

Building a knowledge-sharing culture involves creating an environment where the exchange of information, ideas, and expertise is encouraged and valued. This begins with leadership commitment to modeling and promoting knowledge-sharing behaviors. Leaders must demonstrate the importance of sharing knowledge by actively participating in knowledge-sharing activities and recognizing the contributions of others. This sets the tone for the rest of the organization and emphasizes the value placed on collective intelligence.

Creating formal and informal opportunities for knowledge sharing is essential. This can include structured activities like workshops, training sessions, and regular meetings where employees are encouraged to present their ideas and insights. Informal opportunities, such as social gatherings and casual conversations, also play a crucial role in fostering a knowledge-sharing culture. These interactions help build trust and rapport among employees, making them more likely to share their knowledge.

Incentives and recognition are powerful tools for encouraging knowledge sharing. Recognizing and rewarding employees who contribute to the knowledge base reinforces the importance of these behaviors and motivates others to follow suit. This recognition can take various forms, such as public acknowledgment, awards, or integrating knowledge-sharing metrics into performance evaluations. By tying knowledge sharing to tangible rewards, organizations can emphasize its significance and encourage widespread participation.

Open communication channels are vital for facilitating the flow of knowledge. Implementing digital platforms such as intranets, collaboration tools, and knowledge management systems can make it easier for employees to access and share information. These platforms should be user-friendly and accessible, ensuring that all employees can contribute regardless of their technical proficiency. Encouraging the use of these tools through training and support helps embed them into daily routines.

Creating a safe environment where employees feel comfortable sharing their ideas and experiences without fear of judgment or retribution is crucial. Psychological safety encourages open dialogue and the free exchange of information. Leaders can foster this environment by actively listening to employees, valuing diverse perspectives, and addressing any negative behaviors that might hinder knowledge sharing. Promoting a culture of respect and inclusivity further supports this goal.

Continuous learning and development are key components of a knowledge-sharing culture. Providing employees with opportunities to enhance their skills and knowledge through training programs, workshops, and access to learning resources encourages a growth mindset. This focus on learning helps employees see the value of sharing knowledge and positions them as lifelong learners who contribute to the organization's collective intelligence.

Encouraging cross-functional collaboration helps break down silos and promotes the exchange of knowledge across different areas of the organization. Cross-functional teams bring together diverse expertise and perspectives, leading to more innovative solutions and better decision-making. Facilitating regular interactions between different departments can enhance understanding and cooperation, further embedding knowledge sharing into the organizational culture.

Feedback mechanisms are essential for maintaining and improving knowledge-sharing practices. Regularly soliciting feedback from employees about the effectiveness of knowledge-sharing initiatives and platforms helps identify areas for improvement. This feedback can be used to refine strategies, ensuring that they remain relevant and effective in promoting knowledge sharing.

Building a knowledge-sharing culture requires a multifaceted approach that involves leadership commitment, creating opportunities for sharing, providing incentives and recognition, ensuring open communication, fostering a safe and inclusive environment, promoting continuous learning, encouraging cross-functional collaboration, and implementing effective feedback mechanisms. By embedding these practices into the organizational fabric, leaders can create a dynamic and collaborative environment where knowledge is freely exchanged, driving innovation and supporting overall organizational success.

Inviting team members to be change agents and lifelong learners involves fostering an environment where continuous improvement and personal development are integral to the organizational culture. This starts with leaders who inspire and empower their employees by encouraging them to take ownership of their roles and contribute to the organization's evolution. Leaders should model a commitment to learning and change, demonstrating the importance of staying adaptable and informed in a rapidly changing business landscape.

Creating opportunities for professional growth is essential. Organizations can offer training programs, workshops, and access to online courses that help employees develop new skills and expand their knowledge. Providing resources such as books, articles, and access to industry conferences also supports continuous learning. Encouraging employees to pursue certifications and advanced degrees can further enhance their expertise and contribute to their professional growth.

Mentorship and coaching programs can play a significant role in fostering lifelong learning and change agency. Pairing less experienced employees with seasoned mentors provides guidance, support, and valuable insights into career development. Coaching helps employees set and achieve personal and professional goals, fostering a mindset of continuous improvement.

Encouraging collaboration and knowledge sharing among team members enhances learning and drives innovation. Creating cross-functional teams allows employees to learn from each other's diverse perspectives and experiences, leading to more creative solutions and a deeper understanding of the organization. Regular team meetings, brainstorming sessions, and collaborative projects can facilitate this exchange of ideas.

Recognizing and rewarding efforts to learn and drive change reinforces the value placed on these behaviors. Public acknowledgment of employees who take initiative and contribute to positive change encourages others to do the same. Integrating these values into performance evaluations and career advancement criteria further emphasizes their importance.

Providing a safe and supportive environment is crucial for fostering a culture of lifelong learning and change agency. Employees should feel comfortable experimenting with new ideas and approaches without fear of failure or criticism. Leaders can create this environment by encouraging risk-taking, celebrating successes, and viewing failures as opportunities for learning and growth.

Open communication is vital for inviting team members to be change agents and lifelong learners. Leaders should actively seek feedback and listen to employees' ideas and concerns, demonstrating that their input is valued. This dialogue helps identify areas for improvement and fosters a sense of ownership and engagement among employees.

Promoting a growth mindset throughout the organization encourages employees to view challenges as opportunities to develop their skills and knowledge. Leaders can reinforce this mindset by providing regular feedback, offering constructive criticism, and encouraging employees to set and pursue personal development goals.

Embedding continuous learning and change into the organizational culture requires a holistic approach that includes leadership commitment, professional development opportunities, mentorship, collaboration, recognition, a supportive environment, open communication, and a growth mindset. By fostering these elements, organizations can empower their employees to become proactive change agents and lifelong learners, driving innovation, adaptability, and long-term success.

Chapter 9 has explored the critical role of knowledge management in fostering innovation, improving decision-making, and maintaining a competitive edge in today's rapidly evolving business environment. Effective knowledge management involves creating, sharing, and managing knowledge assets to ensure that valuable information is accessible and usable across the organization. By adopting these strategies, organizations can enhance their efficiency, support continuous improvement, and drive sustainable growth.

We began by discussing strategies for knowledge creation, sharing, and management. Knowledge creation requires fostering an environment that encourages innovation and collaboration, while knowledge sharing involves breaking down silos and promoting transparency. Effective knowledge management ensures that information is organized, easily retrievable, and used to enhance decision-making and problem-solving capabilities.

The role of technology in knowledge management was highlighted as a pivotal factor. Advanced tools and platforms facilitate the seamless integration of knowledge processes, making it easier for employees to capture, store, and share information. Technologies such as document management systems, collaboration tools, artificial intelligence, and data analytics enhance the efficiency and effectiveness of knowledge management, ensuring that knowledge assets are leveraged to their full potential.

Building a knowledge-sharing culture is essential for sustaining effective knowledge management practices. This involves creating an environment where employees are encouraged and rewarded for sharing their expertise and insights. Leaders play a crucial role in fostering this culture by modeling knowledge-sharing behaviors and promoting continuous learning. By cultivating a culture that values knowledge exchange and collaboration, organizations can enhance their collective intelligence and drive ongoing improvement.

Inviting team members to be change agents and lifelong learners is a powerful strategy for embedding knowledge management into the organizational fabric. Encouraging employees to take ownership of their learning and development enhances their individual capabilities and contributes to the organization's overall knowledge base. Providing opportunities for professional growth, mentorship, and collaboration empowers employees to continuously expand their skills and share their knowledge with others.

As we conclude Chapter 9, it is essential to recognize that knowledge management is not a one-time initiative but an ongoing process that requires continuous attention and refinement. By embracing the strategies and principles discussed in this chapter, organizations can create a dynamic and informed environment where knowledge is actively managed and leveraged for maximum impact.

Moving forward, let the insights gained from this chapter inspire you to develop and implement a comprehensive knowledge management strategy that harnesses the power of technology, fosters a culture of learning, and empowers your team members to be proactive agents of change. By doing so, you can ensure that your organization remains at the forefront of innovation and excellence, continually evolving and growing in the face of new challenges and opportunities.

Through dedication to knowledge management and a commitment to fostering a culture of continuous learning and collaboration, you can lead your organization toward sustained success and long-term growth. Embrace these principles to create a more resilient, adaptive, and high-performing organization that thrives in an ever-changing business landscape.

Chapter 10: Collaborative Learning and Technology Strategy

In an increasingly complex and fast-paced business environment, the ability to learn and adapt collaboratively is a critical determinant of organizational success. Chapter 10 delves into the synergy between collaborative learning and technology strategy, emphasizing how these elements can be seamlessly integrated to foster a culture of continuous improvement and innovation. By leveraging the power of collaborative learning and aligning technology with organizational goals, companies can enhance their agility, resilience, and overall performance.

Organizational learning involves creating an environment where employees continuously acquire, share, and apply knowledge to improve their work and drive the organization forward. A crucial aspect of fostering effective organizational learning is cultivating a psychological safety culture. Psychological safety refers to a work environment where individuals feel safe to take risks, voice their opinions, and make mistakes without fear of negative consequences. This culture encourages open dialogue, experimentation, and the free exchange of ideas, which are essential for collaborative learning.

Integrating collaborative learning into the organizational culture involves embedding practices and values that support teamwork, shared knowledge, and collective problem-solving. This integration requires deliberate efforts to break down silos, promote cross-functional collaboration, and create opportunities for employees to learn from each other. By fostering a culture that values and facilitates collaborative learning, organizations can enhance their capacity to innovate and adapt to changing circumstances.

Aligning technology strategy with organizational goals is key to maximizing the impact of collaborative learning initiatives. Technology should not be viewed as an end in itself but as an enabler of strategic objectives. By carefully selecting and implementing technologies that support collaborative learning, organizations can ensure that their technology investments directly contribute to their overall mission and vision. This alignment involves understanding the specific needs of the organization, identifying the right tools and platforms, and integrating these technologies into everyday workflows.

Various tools and platforms can support collaborative learning, ranging from communication and collaboration software to learning management systems and knowledge-sharing platforms. These technologies facilitate real-time collaboration, document sharing, and continuous learning, making it easier for employees to connect, share knowledge, and work together effectively. The right tools can enhance the efficiency and effectiveness of collaborative learning, ensuring that employees have the resources they need to succeed.

As we explore the principles of organizational learning, the importance of a psychological safety culture, strategies for integrating collaborative learning into organizational culture, aligning technology strategy with organizational goals, and the tools and platforms that support collaborative learning, you will gain a comprehensive understanding of how to create a dynamic and innovative learning environment. This chapter will provide practical insights and strategies to help you leverage collaborative learning and technology to drive organizational success.

Let this chapter guide you in developing a cohesive approach to collaborative learning and technology strategy. By fostering a culture of psychological safety, integrating collaborative learning practices, aligning technology with strategic goals, and utilizing effective tools and platforms, you can create a resilient and adaptive organization capable of thriving in an ever-changing business landscape. Embrace these principles to build a learning-oriented, technologically advanced organization that is well-equipped to meet future challenges and seize new opportunities.

Organizational learning is the process through which an organization continuously improves by acquiring, sharing, and applying knowledge. It involves creating a work environment where employees are encouraged to seek out new information, experiment with different approaches, and learn from their experiences and those of their colleagues. This continuous cycle of learning helps organizations adapt to changing conditions, innovate, and maintain a competitive edge.

A critical component of effective organizational learning is the establishment of a psychological safety culture. Psychological safety refers to an environment where employees feel secure in taking risks, voicing their opinions, and admitting mistakes without fear of negative consequences. When individuals feel psychologically safe, they are more likely to engage in open dialogue, share ideas, and collaborate effectively.

In a psychologically safe culture, employees trust that their contributions are valued and that they will not be punished or humiliated for speaking up or making errors. This trust fosters a sense of belonging and encourages employees to participate actively in problem-solving and decision-making processes. Leaders play a crucial role in cultivating psychological safety by modeling inclusive behaviors, actively listening to team members, and demonstrating respect for diverse perspectives.

The interplay between organizational learning and psychological safety is fundamental to creating a high-performing organization. When employees feel safe, they are more likely to engage in behaviors that promote learning, such as asking questions, seeking feedback, and experimenting with new methods. This openness to learning helps organizations continuously improve their processes, products, and services.

To foster organizational learning and psychological safety, it is essential to create opportunities for knowledge sharing and collaboration. This can be achieved through regular team meetings, cross-functional projects, and learning sessions where employees can discuss their experiences and insights. Encouraging a culture of feedback, where constructive criticism is welcomed and used for growth, further supports the development of these essential components.

Organizations that prioritize both organizational learning and psychological safety create an environment where innovation thrives and employees feel empowered to contribute their best work. This combination leads to a more resilient and adaptive organization, capable of navigating the complexities and uncertainties of the modern business landscape. By embedding these principles into the organizational culture, leaders can ensure sustained success and continuous improvement.

Integrating collaborative learning into organizational culture involves creating an environment where teamwork, knowledge sharing, and collective problem-solving are fundamental values. This process starts with leadership commitment to fostering collaboration and recognizing its importance for innovation and continuous improvement. Leaders should model collaborative behaviors, encourage open communication, and actively promote cross-functional teamwork.

Creating opportunities for employees to learn from each other is essential. This can be achieved through structured activities like workshops, training programs, and regular team meetings where employees can share their expertise and insights. Additionally, informal opportunities for collaboration, such as social events and casual discussions, help build relationships and trust among team members, making them more likely to share knowledge and work together effectively.

Encouraging a culture of feedback is crucial for collaborative learning. Regularly seeking and providing feedback helps employees understand their strengths and areas for improvement, fostering a growth mindset. Constructive feedback should be delivered in a supportive manner, focusing on behaviors and outcomes rather than personal attributes. This approach helps build a culture where learning from mistakes and successes is valued.

Providing the necessary tools and resources to support collaboration is also important. Digital platforms like collaboration software, intranets, and knowledge management systems facilitate real-time communication and information sharing. These tools should be user-friendly and accessible to all employees, ensuring that collaboration is seamless and integrated into daily workflows.

Recognizing and rewarding collaborative efforts reinforces the value placed on teamwork and knowledge sharing. Acknowledging employees who actively participate in collaborative learning and contribute to the organization's knowledge base motivates others to do the same. This recognition can take various forms, such as public acknowledgment, awards, or incorporating collaborative behaviors into performance evaluations.

Promoting diversity and inclusivity within teams enhances collaborative learning. Diverse teams bring a range of perspectives and experiences, leading to more innovative solutions and richer discussions. Ensuring that all voices are heard and valued fosters a more inclusive and dynamic learning environment.

Building a culture of trust is fundamental to successful collaboration. Employees need to feel confident that their contributions are respected and that they can rely on their colleagues. Trust is built through consistent, transparent communication, reliability, and mutual support.

Integrating collaborative learning into organizational culture requires ongoing commitment and effort. Leaders must continuously evaluate and refine strategies to ensure they remain effective and aligned with the organization's goals. By embedding collaborative learning into the core values and practices of the organization, leaders can create a dynamic and innovative environment where employees feel empowered to share knowledge and work together towards common objectives. This integration ultimately leads to a more resilient, adaptable, and high-performing organization.

Aligning technology strategy with organizational goals involves ensuring that technological investments and initiatives directly support the broader mission and strategic objectives of the organization. This alignment begins with a clear understanding of the organization's goals and how technology can facilitate achieving them. Leaders must articulate these goals clearly and work closely with IT and other departments to identify the technologies that will best support these objectives.

Integrating technology into strategic planning processes is essential. This means considering technological needs and opportunities as part of the overall business strategy rather than treating them as separate or secondary concerns. By doing so, organizations can ensure that technology initiatives are aligned with key business priorities, such as improving efficiency, enhancing customer experiences, or driving innovation.

Collaboration between business units and IT is crucial for effective alignment. Regular communication and collaboration ensure that technology decisions are informed by a deep understanding of business needs and that IT strategies are flexible and responsive to changing business conditions. This collaborative approach helps bridge the gap between technical capabilities and business requirements, fostering a more integrated and cohesive strategy.

Investing in technologies that offer scalability and flexibility is vital. Organizations should prioritize tools and platforms that can grow and adapt with the business, supporting both current operations and future expansion. This forward-thinking approach ensures that technological investments continue to deliver value as the organization evolves.

Ongoing assessment and refinement of the technology strategy are necessary to maintain alignment with organizational goals. This involves regularly reviewing technological initiatives to ensure they are delivering the expected benefits and making adjustments as needed. Feedback loops, performance metrics, and continuous improvement practices help keep the strategy aligned with changing business needs and emerging opportunities.

Education and training are important components of aligning technology strategy with organizational goals. Ensuring that employees understand and can effectively use new technologies is crucial for maximizing their potential. Providing ongoing training and support helps build the skills needed to leverage technology effectively, driving better outcomes and supporting strategic objectives.

Leadership commitment to aligning technology strategy with organizational goals is essential. Leaders must champion the integration of technology and business strategies, demonstrating the importance of this alignment through their actions and decisions. By fostering a culture that values technological innovation and strategic alignment, leaders can ensure that technology investments drive meaningful business results.

Aligning technology strategy with organizational goals involves a comprehensive and ongoing effort to integrate technological initiatives with the broader business strategy. This alignment supports the organization in achieving its strategic objectives, driving innovation, and maintaining a competitive edge. By prioritizing collaboration, flexibility, continuous assessment, and leadership commitment, organizations can harness the full potential of technology to achieve sustained success.

Tools and platforms for collaborative learning play a crucial role in facilitating communication, knowledge sharing, and teamwork within organizations. These technologies provide the infrastructure necessary for employees to work together effectively, regardless of their physical location. Collaborative learning tools include communication platforms such as video conferencing software, which enables real-time interactions and meetings, and instant messaging applications that allow for quick, informal exchanges of information. These tools help maintain a continuous flow of communication, essential for collaborative efforts.

Document management systems are vital for organizing and sharing information. These platforms allow team members to create, edit, and store documents in a centralized location, making it easy for everyone to access and collaborate on the same files. Features such as version control and real-time editing ensure that all team members are working with the most current information, reducing confusion and errors.

Project management tools help coordinate tasks and track progress. These platforms provide a structured way to assign tasks, set deadlines, and monitor the status of projects. By offering visual dashboards and automated reminders, project management tools help teams stay organized and ensure that collaborative efforts are aligned with project goals and timelines.

Learning management systems (LMS) support the delivery and management of educational content. These platforms facilitate the creation, distribution, and tracking of training programs and learning materials. An LMS can include features such as online courses, quizzes, and discussion forums, enabling employees to engage in collaborative learning at their own pace. The ability to track progress and performance helps organizations ensure that learning objectives are being met.

Knowledge sharing platforms, such as wikis and internal social networks, provide spaces for employees to contribute and access organizational knowledge. These platforms allow team members to post articles, share best practices, and discuss ideas, creating a repository of collective knowledge. By making it easy to find and share information, these tools support ongoing learning and collaboration.

Cloud-based collaboration tools offer flexibility and accessibility. These platforms enable employees to work together on documents, spreadsheets, and presentations from any location with internet access. Cloud storage ensures that files are always up-to-date and can be accessed by authorized team members, facilitating seamless collaboration and data sharing.

Analytics tools help organizations measure the effectiveness of collaborative learning initiatives. By tracking usage patterns, engagement levels, and learning outcomes, these tools provide insights into how collaborative learning efforts are impacting performance. This data can inform decisions about future investments in learning technologies and strategies.

Incorporating these tools and platforms into the organizational workflow requires careful planning and integration. It is essential to select technologies that align with the organization's needs and goals, ensuring that they enhance rather than disrupt existing processes. Providing training and support for employees on how to use these tools effectively is crucial for maximizing their benefits.

Tools and platforms for collaborative learning are essential for fostering communication, knowledge sharing, and teamwork within organizations. By utilizing communication platforms, document management systems, project management tools, learning management systems, knowledge sharing platforms, cloud-based collaboration tools, and analytics tools, organizations can create an environment that supports continuous learning and collaboration. These technologies enable employees to work together more effectively, driving innovation and achieving organizational goals.

Chapter 10 has explored the powerful synergy between collaborative learning and technology strategy, highlighting how these elements can be integrated to foster a culture of continuous improvement and innovation. By leveraging the right tools and platforms, organizations can enhance their capacity for learning and adaptation, ensuring they remain competitive and resilient in an ever-changing business environment.

We began by discussing the principles of organizational learning and the importance of a psychological safety culture. These concepts form the foundation for effective collaborative learning, as they create an environment where employees feel safe to share ideas, take risks, and learn from both successes and failures. A psychologically safe workplace encourages open dialogue and the free exchange of knowledge, which are essential for fostering innovation and continuous improvement.

Integrating collaborative learning into the organizational culture involves creating opportunities for teamwork, shared knowledge, and collective problem-solving. This requires deliberate efforts to break down silos, promote cross-functional collaboration, and encourage employees to learn from each other. By embedding collaborative learning practices into the core values and daily operations of the organization, leaders can create a dynamic and innovative environment that supports sustained growth and success.

Aligning technology strategy with organizational goals is crucial for maximizing the impact of collaborative learning initiatives. Technology should be seen as an enabler of strategic objectives, not just a set of tools. By carefully selecting and implementing technologies that support collaborative learning, organizations can ensure that their technology investments directly contribute to their overall mission and vision. This alignment involves ongoing collaboration between business units and IT, ensuring that technological solutions are flexible, scalable, and responsive to changing business needs.

The role of tools and platforms for collaborative learning cannot be overstated. Communication platforms, document management systems, project management tools, learning management systems, knowledge sharing platforms, cloud-based collaboration tools, and analytics tools all play a vital role in facilitating real-time collaboration, organizing information, and measuring the effectiveness of learning initiatives. These technologies make it easier for employees to connect, share knowledge, and work together effectively, driving better outcomes and supporting strategic goals.

As we conclude Chapter 10, it is essential to recognize that the integration of collaborative learning and technology strategy is an ongoing process that requires continuous attention and refinement. By fostering a culture of psychological safety, embedding collaborative learning practices into the organizational culture, aligning technology with strategic goals, and utilizing effective tools and platforms, leaders can create a resilient and adaptive organization capable of thriving in an ever-changing business landscape.

Moving forward, let the insights and strategies discussed in this chapter inspire you to develop a comprehensive approach to collaborative learning and technology strategy. By embracing these principles, you can build a learning-oriented, technologically advanced organization that is well-equipped to meet future challenges and seize new opportunities. Through dedication to continuous improvement and a commitment to fostering a collaborative and innovative culture, you can lead your organization toward sustained success and long-term growth.

Part III: Global Perspectives and Corporate Responsibility

Organizations must navigate a complex web of global dynamics and responsibilities. Part III of this book, "Global Perspectives and Corporate Responsibility," explores how businesses can effectively manage these challenges while upholding ethical standards and contributing positively to society. This section delves into the trends shaping global labor markets, the importance of corporate social responsibility (CSR), the critical role of diversity and inclusion, and the transformative power of leadership in driving meaningful change.

Chapter 11: Global Labor Markets

Global labor markets are evolving rapidly, influenced by technological advancements, economic shifts, and demographic changes. In this chapter, we will examine the latest trends and challenges that organizations face in managing a global workforce. We will explore strategies for navigating these complexities, including effective talent management, cultural adaptation, and compliance with international labor laws. Understanding these dynamics is crucial for organizations aiming to leverage global talent and remain competitive in a diverse and fluid labor market.

Chapter 12: Corporate Social Responsibility (CSR)

Corporate Social Responsibility has become a cornerstone of modern business practice. This chapter highlights the importance of CSR in building sustainable and ethical organizations. We will discuss how to implement and measure CSR initiatives, ensuring they align with organizational goals and stakeholder expectations. By integrating CSR into their core strategies, organizations can enhance their reputation, foster customer loyalty, and contribute to societal well-being. Practical examples and case studies will illustrate the benefits and challenges of effective CSR implementation.

Chapter 13: Social Justice, Diversity, and Inclusion

Promoting diversity and inclusion is not only a moral imperative but also a strategic advantage. This chapter focuses on strategies for fostering an inclusive workplace that values diverse perspectives and promotes social justice. We will explore policies and practices that support diversity, equity, and inclusion, helping organizations to build a more dynamic and innovative workforce. Additionally, we will examine the role of organizational policies in advancing social justice, ensuring that all employees have equal opportunities to thrive.

Chapter 14: Transformational Leadership Methods

Transformational leadership is essential for guiding organizations through periods of change and uncertainty. This chapter delves into the characteristics of transformational leaders and the skills required to develop this leadership style. We will explore how transformational leaders can inspire and motivate their teams, driving significant organizational change. The impact of transformational leadership on organizational culture and performance will be examined, highlighting the critical role leaders play in fostering a resilient and forward-thinking organization.

Part III of this book provides a comprehensive overview of the global perspectives and responsibilities that modern organizations must embrace. By understanding and addressing the challenges of global labor markets, committing to corporate social responsibility, promoting diversity and inclusion, and cultivating transformational leadership, organizations can navigate the complexities of the global business environment. This section equips readers with the knowledge and tools needed to build ethical, inclusive, and sustainable organizations that are well-positioned for long-term success.

Chapter 11: Global Labor Markets

Understanding the dynamics of global labor markets has become essential for organizations seeking to thrive in the international arena. Chapter 11 explores the complexities and opportunities presented by global labor markets, providing insights into the trends, challenges, and strategies for managing a diverse and geographically dispersed workforce. As businesses expand their operations across borders, leaders must navigate a myriad of economic, cultural, and regulatory landscapes to harness the full potential of their global teams.

Globalism reflects the profound changes and advancements that have shaped the way organizations operate on an international scale. Technological innovations, shifting economic power, and evolving social norms have transformed the global workforce, creating both opportunities and challenges for businesses. Organizations must stay abreast of these changes to remain competitive and effectively leverage the diverse talents available in different regions.

Trends and challenges in global labor markets are multifaceted. On one hand, technological advancements such as artificial intelligence, automation, and digital platforms are reshaping job roles and demand for skills. On the other hand, geopolitical tensions, economic disparities, and cultural differences present significant hurdles. Organizations must navigate these complexities while addressing issues such as talent shortages, remote work, and employee well-being. Recognizing these trends and challenges is crucial for developing strategies that can turn potential obstacles into opportunities for growth and innovation.

Managing a global workforce requires strategic approaches that take into account the diverse needs and expectations of employees across different regions. This involves implementing flexible work arrangements, fostering an inclusive organizational culture, and ensuring compliance with various legal and regulatory requirements. Effective communication and collaboration tools are essential for bridging geographical distances and enabling seamless interaction among team members. Additionally, investing in employee development and creating opportunities for cross-cultural learning can enhance the overall effectiveness of a global workforce.

Leadership in a global economy demands a nuanced understanding of diverse cultural contexts and the ability to inspire and guide teams across borders. Global leaders must be adept at navigating cultural differences, building trust, and fostering collaboration among team members from varied backgrounds. This requires cultural intelligence, adaptability, and a commitment to continuous learning. By developing these skills, leaders can create a cohesive and motivated global workforce that drives organizational success in a competitive international landscape.

As we delve into the intricacies of global labor markets, this chapter will provide practical insights and strategies for managing and leading a global workforce. From understanding the impact of globalism to addressing the trends and challenges in international labor markets, you will gain the knowledge and tools needed to navigate the complexities of operating on a global scale. By embracing these principles, you can position your organization for success in the dynamic and ever-evolving global economy.

Globalism is characterized by the accelerated integration of economies, cultures, and technologies across the world. Technological innovations have drastically reshaped how businesses operate, enabling seamless communication and collaboration across borders. Digital platforms, artificial intelligence, and automation are driving efficiency and creating new opportunities for growth. These advancements have also led to the emergence of new industries and job roles, requiring a workforce that is adaptable and skilled in cutting-edge technologies.

Economic power is shifting, with emerging markets gaining prominence on the global stage. Countries in Asia, Africa, and Latin America are experiencing rapid economic growth, attracting investments and expanding their influence. This shift is creating a more multipolar world where businesses must navigate a diverse array of markets and regulatory environments. Global trade continues to be a driving force, but it is increasingly influenced by geopolitical tensions and trade policies that can affect supply chains and market access.

Cultural exchange and diversity are at the forefront of globalism. The global workforce is more interconnected than ever, with employees from different backgrounds and regions working together. This diversity brings a wealth of perspectives and ideas, fostering innovation and creativity. However, it also requires organizations to be culturally sensitive and adept at managing cross-cultural teams. Inclusivity and cultural intelligence are becoming essential competencies for leaders and employees alike.

The rise of remote work has further transformed the global labor market. The COVID-19 pandemic accelerated the adoption of remote work, and it has since become a permanent fixture for many organizations. This shift allows companies to tap into a global talent pool, but it also presents challenges in terms of managing remote teams, ensuring cybersecurity, and maintaining employee engagement. Flexible work arrangements and robust digital infrastructure are crucial for supporting this new way of working.

Sustainability and corporate responsibility are increasingly important in the global landscape. Consumers and stakeholders are demanding that companies operate ethically and sustainably, considering the environmental and social impacts of their actions. Businesses are adopting sustainable practices and integrating corporate social responsibility into their strategies to meet these expectations and contribute to global efforts to address climate change and social inequality.

Globalism is marked by rapid technological advancements, shifting economic power, cultural diversity, the rise of remote work, and a growing emphasis on sustainability. Organizations must navigate these complex and interconnected trends to succeed in the global economy. By embracing innovation, fostering inclusivity, and committing to sustainable practices, businesses can thrive in this dynamic environment and capitalize on the opportunities presented by global integration.

The global labor market is shaped by several key trends, challenges, and opportunities that organizations must navigate to remain competitive. Technological advancements continue to drive significant changes in job roles and skill requirements. Automation and artificial intelligence are transforming industries, leading to the creation of new jobs while rendering others obsolete. This technological shift necessitates a workforce that is adaptable and skilled in emerging technologies.

Economic disparities across regions present both challenges and opportunities. While emerging markets in Asia, Africa, and Latin America are experiencing rapid growth, attracting investments and expanding their influence, developed economies are facing slower growth and aging populations. This economic divergence requires organizations to tailor their strategies to diverse market conditions, capitalizing on growth opportunities in emerging markets while addressing the challenges of stagnation in more mature economies.

The rise of remote work, accelerated by the COVID-19 pandemic, has permanently altered the global labor landscape. Organizations now have access to a global talent pool, allowing them to hire the best talent regardless of geographic location. However, managing a remote workforce presents challenges related to communication, cybersecurity, and maintaining employee engagement. Ensuring that remote work infrastructure is robust and secure is essential for leveraging the benefits of a distributed workforce.

Cultural diversity within the global workforce brings both benefits and challenges. A diverse workforce fosters innovation and creativity by incorporating a wide range of perspectives and ideas. However, it also requires organizations to be culturally sensitive and adept at managing cross-cultural teams. Leaders and employees must develop cultural intelligence to navigate differences effectively and create an inclusive work environment.

Geopolitical tensions and trade policies are significant factors influencing global labor markets. Trade wars, tariffs, and political instability can disrupt supply chains and affect market access. Organizations must stay informed about geopolitical developments and adapt their strategies to mitigate risks and capitalize on opportunities in different regions.

Sustainability and corporate social responsibility are increasingly important in the global labor market. Consumers and stakeholders are demanding that companies operate ethically and sustainably, considering the environmental and social impacts of their actions. Organizations that integrate sustainable practices into their operations can enhance their reputation, attract talent, and meet regulatory requirements.

Talent shortages and skills gaps are ongoing challenges in the global labor market. As technology evolves, there is a growing demand for specialized skills that are in short supply. Organizations must invest in training and development to upskill their existing workforce and attract new talent. Partnerships with educational institutions and continuous learning initiatives can help bridge the skills gap and ensure a steady pipeline of qualified professionals.

The global labor market is influenced by technological advancements, economic disparities, the rise of remote work, cultural diversity, geopolitical tensions, and a focus on sustainability. These trends present both challenges and opportunities for organizations. By staying agile, investing in technology and talent, fostering an inclusive culture, and committing to sustainable practices, businesses can navigate the complexities of the global labor market and position themselves for long-term success.

Effectively managing a global workforce involves implementing strategies that address the diverse needs and expectations of employees across different regions. Creating a flexible work environment is essential. This includes offering remote work options and flexible hours to accommodate different time zones and personal commitments. Flexibility helps to attract and retain top talent from around the world, ensuring that employees can work in ways that suit them best.

Investing in robust communication and collaboration tools is crucial for managing a geographically dispersed team. Technologies such as video conferencing, instant messaging, and project management platforms enable seamless communication and collaboration, helping team members stay connected and work efficiently despite physical distances. Ensuring that these tools are user-friendly and accessible to all employees enhances their effectiveness.

Building a strong organizational culture that transcends geographic boundaries is important for fostering a sense of unity and shared purpose among global employees. This can be achieved by promoting the company's core values and vision consistently across all locations. Regular virtual meetings, team-building activities, and social events can help strengthen relationships and create a cohesive team environment.

Providing training and development opportunities is key to managing a global workforce. Organizations should offer programs that help employees enhance their skills and advance their careers, regardless of their location. This includes online courses, webinars, and access to learning resources. Investing in employee development not only improves performance but also increases job satisfaction and retention.

Ensuring compliance with local laws and regulations is a critical aspect of managing a global workforce. Organizations must be aware of and adhere to labor laws, tax requirements, and employment regulations in each country where they operate. This requires collaboration with legal and HR experts to navigate the complexities of different regulatory environments and avoid potential legal issues.

Fostering an inclusive and culturally sensitive work environment is essential for managing a diverse global team. Leaders should promote cultural awareness and sensitivity, encouraging employees to respect and appreciate different perspectives and backgrounds. Providing diversity and inclusion training helps employees develop the skills needed to work effectively in a multicultural setting.

Implementing consistent performance management practices across all locations ensures that employees are evaluated fairly and objectively. This includes setting clear expectations, providing regular feedback, and conducting performance reviews based on standardized criteria. Consistent performance management helps to align individual goals with organizational objectives and ensures that all employees are held to the same standards.

Offering competitive compensation and benefits packages that are tailored to local markets is important for attracting and retaining global talent. Organizations should benchmark their compensation against industry standards in each region and provide benefits that meet the specific needs of their employees. This might include health insurance, retirement plans, and wellness programs.

Encouraging open communication and feedback is crucial for managing a global workforce. Employees should feel comfortable sharing their ideas, concerns, and suggestions with leadership. Regular surveys, feedback sessions, and open-door policies help to create a transparent and supportive work environment where employees feel valued and heard.

Strategies for managing a global workforce involve creating a flexible work environment, investing in communication and collaboration tools, building a strong organizational culture, providing training and development opportunities, ensuring compliance with local laws, fostering inclusivity, implementing consistent performance management practices, offering competitive compensation, and encouraging open communication. By adopting these strategies, organizations can effectively manage their global workforce, driving engagement, performance, and overall success.

Leadership in a global economy requires a nuanced understanding of diverse cultural contexts and the ability to inspire and guide teams across borders. Effective global leaders must possess cultural intelligence, which involves being aware of and sensitive to cultural differences, and adapting their leadership style accordingly. This capability enables leaders to build trust and foster collaboration among team members from various backgrounds.

Communication skills are paramount for global leaders. They must be adept at conveying their vision and goals clearly and consistently across different regions, using various communication channels to reach their audience effectively. Ensuring that messages are understood in the intended manner requires not only linguistic proficiency but also an understanding of cultural nuances and non-verbal cues.

Flexibility and adaptability are essential traits for global leaders. The dynamic nature of the global economy demands that leaders quickly respond to changing market conditions, technological advancements, and geopolitical shifts. This involves being open to new ideas, willing to pivot strategies, and continuously seeking innovative solutions to complex problems.

Strategic thinking is critical for navigating the complexities of the global economy. Leaders must have a long-term vision and the ability to foresee and plan for future challenges and opportunities. This strategic mindset helps them align organizational goals with global market trends and make informed decisions that drive sustainable growth.

Empathy and emotional intelligence play a significant role in global leadership. Understanding and valuing the emotions and perspectives of team members enhances relationships and fosters a supportive work environment. Leaders who show empathy are better equipped to motivate their teams, manage conflicts, and create an inclusive culture where everyone feels respected and valued.

Building strong networks is another crucial aspect of global leadership. Establishing relationships with key stakeholders, including employees, customers, partners, and industry influencers, helps leaders gain insights, influence outcomes, and drive collaborative efforts. These networks provide support and resources that are invaluable in navigating the global business landscape.

Commitment to continuous learning is vital for leaders in a global economy. The fast-paced and ever-evolving nature of global markets requires leaders to stay updated on industry trends, emerging technologies, and best practices. This ongoing learning enables them to lead with knowledge and confidence, making well-informed decisions that benefit their organizations.

Ethical leadership is imperative in a global context. Leaders must uphold high standards of integrity, transparency, and social responsibility, ensuring that their actions reflect the organization's values and build trust with stakeholders. Ethical conduct not only enhances the organization's reputation but also fosters a culture of accountability and respect.

Innovation and creativity are essential for driving success in the global economy. Leaders must encourage a culture of experimentation and risk-taking, where new ideas are welcomed and explored. By fostering an environment that supports innovation, leaders can drive their organizations to develop unique solutions and maintain a competitive edge.

Leadership in a global economy involves understanding and adapting to cultural differences, effective communication, flexibility, strategic thinking, empathy, building networks, continuous learning, ethical conduct, and fostering innovation.

These qualities enable leaders to inspire and guide their teams across borders, navigate the complexities of the global market, and drive sustainable success for their organizations. Through these efforts, global leaders can ensure their organizations remain resilient, adaptive, and well-positioned for future growth.

Chapter 11 has explored the complexities and opportunities of global labor markets, highlighting the significance of globalism, current trends, challenges, and strategies for managing and leading a global workforce. By understanding these dynamics, organizations can better navigate the intricacies of operating on an international scale and leverage the diverse talents available worldwide.

We began by discussing the concept of globalism in 2024, emphasizing the profound changes brought about by technological advancements, shifting economic power, and increasing cultural diversity. These factors have reshaped the global labor market, creating both opportunities and challenges that organizations must address to remain competitive.

The trends and challenges in global labor markets are multifaceted, encompassing technological advancements, economic disparities, the rise of remote work, cultural diversity, geopolitical tensions, and sustainability. Recognizing these trends is crucial for developing strategies that turn potential obstacles into opportunities for growth and innovation.

Managing a global workforce requires strategic approaches that account for the diverse needs and expectations of employees across different regions. This involves creating flexible work environments, investing in robust communication tools, building a strong organizational culture, providing training and development opportunities, ensuring compliance with local laws, fostering inclusivity, implementing consistent performance management practices, and offering competitive compensation packages. These strategies help organizations attract and retain top talent, enhance employee engagement, and drive overall success.

Leadership in a global economy demands a nuanced understanding of diverse cultural contexts and the ability to inspire and guide teams across borders. Effective global leaders must possess cultural intelligence, strong communication skills, flexibility, strategic thinking, empathy, the ability to build strong networks, a commitment to continuous learning, ethical conduct, and a focus on innovation. These qualities enable leaders to navigate the complexities of the global market, foster collaboration, and drive sustainable success for their organizations.

It is essential to recognize that succeeding in the global labor market requires continuous learning, adaptability, and a commitment to fostering a diverse and inclusive work environment. By embracing the principles and strategies discussed in this chapter, organizations can position themselves for long-term success in an increasingly interconnected and dynamic global economy.

Moving forward, let the insights gained from this chapter inspire you to develop and implement effective strategies for managing and leading a global workforce. By staying agile, investing in technology and talent, fostering an inclusive culture, and committing to ethical and sustainable practices, you can navigate the complexities of the global labor market and achieve sustained growth and success. Embrace these principles to build a resilient, adaptive, and high-performing organization that thrives in the face of global challenges and opportunities.

Chapter 12: Corporate Social Responsibility (CSR)

Corporate Social Responsibility (CSR) has emerged as a vital component of modern organizational strategy. Chapter 12 delves into the concept of CSR, exploring its significance in today's business landscape, the process of developing effective CSR initiatives, and the methodologies for implementing and measuring their success. As stakeholders—ranging from consumers to investors—demand greater transparency and ethical conduct, organizations must integrate CSR into their core operations to foster trust, enhance reputation, and contribute positively to the world.

Corporate Social Responsibility refers to a company's commitment to operate in an economically, socially, and environmentally sustainable manner. This goes beyond compliance with legal requirements and involves voluntary actions that benefit society and the environment. CSR encompasses a wide range of activities, including environmental stewardship, ethical labor practices, philanthropy, and community engagement. In modern organizations, CSR is not just a moral obligation but also a strategic imperative that can drive business success by aligning company values with those of stakeholders.

The importance of CSR in modern organizations cannot be overstated. It enhances corporate reputation, builds consumer trust, and can lead to competitive advantages. Consumers today are more informed and concerned about the ethical implications of their purchases, preferring to support companies that demonstrate a commitment to social and environmental causes. Similarly, employees are increasingly seeking to work for organizations that reflect their own values, making CSR a key factor in attracting and retaining talent. Furthermore, investors are considering CSR performance as a criterion for investment, recognizing that responsible companies are more likely to mitigate risks and achieve long-term profitability.

Developing CSR initiatives requires a strategic approach that aligns with the company's mission, values, and business goals. The first step is conducting a thorough assessment to identify the social and environmental issues that are most relevant to the organization and its stakeholders. Engaging with stakeholders through surveys, interviews, and focus groups can provide valuable insights into their expectations and priorities. Once these issues are identified, organizations can set clear, measurable objectives and develop initiatives that address these areas. Effective CSR initiatives are those that integrate seamlessly into the company's operations and leverage its unique strengths and resources.

Implementing CSR initiatives involves embedding these strategies into the fabric of the organization. This requires commitment from top leadership, clear communication of goals and expectations, and the allocation of necessary resources. Employees at all levels should be engaged and empowered to contribute to CSR efforts, fostering a culture of responsibility and accountability. Partnerships with non-profits, community organizations, and other stakeholders can enhance the impact of CSR initiatives, providing additional expertise and resources.

Measuring the success of CSR initiatives is crucial for demonstrating their value and ensuring continuous improvement. Organizations can use various metrics and reporting frameworks, such as the Global Reporting Initiative (GRI) or the Sustainability Accounting Standards Board (SASB), to track performance against their objectives. Regular monitoring and evaluation help identify areas for improvement and highlight successes that can be communicated to stakeholders. Transparent reporting not only builds credibility but also provides a basis for setting more ambitious goals and advancing CSR efforts.

As we explore the concept, development, implementation, and measurement of CSR, this chapter will provide practical insights and strategies for integrating social responsibility into your organization. By embracing CSR, companies can not only contribute positively to society and the environment but also enhance their own sustainability and success. Through a commitment to responsible business practices, organizations can build stronger relationships with stakeholders, drive innovation, and create long-term value.

Corporate Social Responsibility (CSR) is a company's commitment to operate in an economically, socially, and environmentally sustainable manner. This commitment goes beyond merely complying with legal requirements and involves voluntary actions that benefit society and the environment. CSR encompasses a broad range of activities, including environmental stewardship, ethical labor practices, philanthropy, and community engagement. Modern organizations recognize that CSR is not just a moral obligation but also a strategic imperative that can drive business success by aligning company values with those of stakeholders.

The importance of CSR in modern organizations is multifaceted. It enhances corporate reputation and builds consumer trust, which can lead to competitive advantages. Today's consumers are more informed and concerned about the ethical implications of their purchases. They prefer to support companies that demonstrate a commitment to social and environmental causes. This shift in consumer behavior means that companies with strong CSR practices can attract and retain loyal customers.

CSR also plays a crucial role in employee engagement and retention. Increasingly, employees are seeking to work for organizations that reflect their own values. A robust CSR program can make a company more attractive to potential employees and help retain existing staff by fostering a sense of pride and purpose in their work. This alignment of values between employer and employee can lead to higher job satisfaction and productivity.

From an investor's perspective, CSR performance is becoming an important criterion for investment decisions. Investors recognize that companies with responsible practices are more likely to mitigate risks and achieve long-term profitability. By integrating CSR into their business strategy, organizations can attract investment from those who prioritize ethical and sustainable business practices. Furthermore, CSR initiatives can drive innovation. By addressing social and environmental challenges, companies can identify new market opportunities and develop innovative products and services that meet the evolving needs of society. This proactive approach not only contributes to the greater good but also positions the company as a leader in its industry.

In addition to these benefits, CSR helps companies build stronger relationships with their stakeholders, including customers, employees, investors, and the communities in which they operate. Transparent and responsible business practices foster trust and loyalty, which are essential for long-term success. By engaging in CSR activities, organizations can demonstrate their commitment to making a positive impact, thereby enhancing their overall sustainability and resilience.

CSR is a vital component of modern organizational strategy that involves voluntary actions to benefit society and the environment. It enhances reputation, builds consumer trust, attracts and retains employees, appeals to investors, drives innovation, and strengthens stakeholder relationships. By integrating CSR into their operations, companies can achieve sustainable success and contribute positively to the world around them.

Developing Corporate Social Responsibility (CSR) initiatives involves a strategic approach that aligns with the company's mission, values, and business goals. The process begins with a thorough assessment to identify the social and environmental issues most relevant to the organization and its stakeholders. This assessment can include engaging with stakeholders through surveys, interviews, and focus groups to gain insights into their expectations and priorities. Once these key issues are identified, the organization can set clear, measurable objectives that address these areas.

Crafting effective CSR initiatives requires integrating them into the company's core operations and leveraging its unique strengths and resources. This means identifying how the company can make the most significant impact while also benefiting from these activities. For instance, a technology firm might focus on digital literacy programs, while a manufacturing company could prioritize reducing its environmental footprint.

Collaboration is a vital element in developing successful CSR initiatives. Partnering with non-profits, community organizations, and other stakeholders can enhance the reach and impact of CSR efforts. These partnerships provide additional expertise, resources, and credibility to the initiatives, ensuring they are well-rounded and effective.

Communication is crucial throughout the development process. Internally, it's important to engage employees at all levels to foster a sense of ownership and involvement in CSR activities. This can be achieved through workshops, meetings, and internal communications that highlight the importance and benefits of CSR. Externally, transparent communication about the company's CSR goals and progress builds trust and demonstrates accountability to stakeholders.

Innovative thinking can also play a significant role in developing CSR initiatives. Encouraging creative solutions to social and environmental challenges can lead to groundbreaking programs that set the company apart as a leader in sustainability and responsibility. This innovation can be driven by creating a culture that values and rewards proactive problem-solving and social impact.

To ensure CSR initiatives are sustainable and impactful, it's essential to establish metrics for success. These metrics should be tied to the organization's broader strategic goals and provide a clear framework for assessing the effectiveness of CSR activities. Regular monitoring and evaluation of these metrics allow the company to make data-driven decisions, adjust strategies as needed, and continuously improve the initiatives.

Developing CSR initiatives involves identifying relevant issues, setting measurable objectives, integrating efforts into core operations, collaborating with partners, engaging stakeholders, fostering innovation, and establishing success metrics. By adopting this comprehensive approach, organizations can create meaningful and effective CSR programs that align with their business goals and contribute positively to society and the environment. Increasing Corporate Social Responsibility (CSR) initiatives involves a strategic approach that aligns with the company's mission, values, and business goals. The process begins with a thorough assessment to identify the social and environmental issues most relevant to the organization and its stakeholders. Engaging with stakeholders through surveys, interviews, and focus groups provides valuable insights into their expectations and priorities. Once these key issues are identified, the organization can set clear, measurable objectives that address these areas.

Crafting effective CSR initiatives requires integrating them into the company's core operations and leveraging its unique strengths and resources. Identifying how the company can make the most significant impact while also benefiting from these activities is crucial. For example, a technology firm might focus on digital literacy programs, while a manufacturing company could prioritize reducing its environmental footprint.

Collaboration is a vital element in developing successful CSR initiatives. Partnering with non-profits, community organizations, and other stakeholders can enhance the reach and impact of CSR efforts. These partnerships provide additional expertise, resources, and credibility, ensuring the initiatives are well-rounded and effective.

Communication is crucial throughout the development process. Internally, engaging employees at all levels fosters a sense of ownership and involvement in CSR activities. This can be achieved through workshops, meetings, and internal communications that highlight the importance and benefits of CSR. Externally, transparent communication about the company's

CSR goals and progress builds trust and demonstrates accountability to stakeholders.

Innovative thinking also plays a significant role in developing CSR initiatives. Encouraging creative solutions to social and environmental challenges can lead to groundbreaking programs that set the company apart as a leader in sustainability and responsibility. Creating a culture that values and rewards proactive problem-solving and social impact can drive this innovation.

Establishing metrics for success ensures CSR initiatives are sustainable and impactful. These metrics should be tied to the organization's broader strategic goals and provide a clear framework for assessing the effectiveness of CSR activities. Regular monitoring and evaluation of these metrics allow the company to make data-driven decisions, adjust strategies as needed, and continuously improve the initiatives.

Developing CSR initiatives involves identifying relevant issues, setting measurable objectives, integrating efforts into core operations, collaborating with partners, engaging stakeholders, fostering innovation, and establishing success metrics. By adopting this comprehensive approach, organizations can create meaningful and effective CSR programs that align with their business goals and contribute positively to society and the environment.

Implementing CSR initiatives involves embedding these strategies into the organization's operations and ensuring they are embraced by all levels of the company. This process starts with a strong commitment from top leadership, as their support and involvement are crucial for driving the initiatives forward. Clear communication of CSR goals and expectations to employees fosters understanding and buy-in, creating a unified effort towards achieving the set objectives.

Allocating the necessary resources, including time, budget, and personnel, is essential for the successful implementation of CSR initiatives. This includes designating teams or individuals responsible for overseeing the projects and ensuring they have the skills and tools needed to execute their tasks effectively. Regular training and development opportunities help equip employees with the knowledge and capabilities required to contribute to CSR efforts.

Engaging employees across the organization is critical for embedding CSR into the company culture. Encouraging participation through volunteer programs, internal campaigns, and collaborative projects helps to build a sense of ownership and commitment among staff. Celebrating successes and recognizing contributions further motivates employees and reinforces the importance of CSR.

Partnerships with external organizations, such as non-profits and community groups, can enhance the impact of CSR initiatives. These collaborations bring additional expertise and resources, expanding the reach and effectiveness of the projects. Working closely with partners ensures that initiatives are aligned with broader societal goals and address relevant issues effectively.

Measuring the success of CSR initiatives is crucial for demonstrating their value and ensuring continuous improvement. Establishing clear metrics and key performance indicators (KPIs) allows organizations to track progress against their objectives. These metrics should cover various aspects of the initiatives, including environmental impact, social contributions, and economic benefits.

Regular monitoring and evaluation of CSR activities provide insights into what is working well and where adjustments may be needed. This process involves collecting data, analyzing results, and seeking feedback from stakeholders to understand the outcomes and impact of the initiatives. Transparent reporting of these findings builds credibility and trust with stakeholders, showing a commitment to accountability and continuous improvement.

Using recognized frameworks and standards, such as the Global Reporting Initiative (GRI) or the Sustainability Accounting Standards Board (SASB), helps organizations benchmark their performance and align with industry best practices. These frameworks provide guidance on how to measure and report CSR activities, ensuring consistency and comparability.

Implementing and measuring CSR initiatives requires embedding strategies into the organization's operations with leadership commitment, resource allocation, employee engagement, and external partnerships. Establishing clear metrics and regularly monitoring and evaluating activities ensures continuous improvement and transparency. By adopting these practices, organizations can effectively implement CSR initiatives that drive positive social and environmental impact while contributing to their overall success.

Chapter 12 has explored the integral role of Corporate Social Responsibility (CSR) in modern organizations, emphasizing its importance, development, implementation, and measurement. As businesses navigate the complexities of the 21st century, CSR has emerged as a vital strategy for aligning company operations with societal and environmental values, enhancing reputation, and driving long-term success. We began by defining CSR and discussing its significance. CSR involves voluntary actions that benefit society and the environment, extending beyond mere legal compliance. It enhances corporate reputation, builds consumer trust, attracts and retains employees, appeals to investors, drives innovation, and strengthens stakeholder relationships. In essence, CSR is not just about doing good; it is about doing well by doing good.

Developing CSR initiatives requires a strategic and integrated approach. Organizations must start with a thorough assessment to identify the most relevant social and environmental issues, engage stakeholders to understand their priorities, and set clear, measurable objectives. Effective CSR initiatives leverage the company's unique strengths and resources, foster innovation, and include partnerships with non-profits and community organizations. Communication, both internal and external, plays a crucial role in ensuring that these initiatives are understood, supported, and celebrated.

Implementing CSR initiatives involves embedding them into the fabric of the organization with strong leadership commitment, resource allocation, and active employee engagement. Training, development, and collaboration are key elements that empower employees to contribute meaningfully to CSR efforts. Engaging external partners enhances the reach and impact of these initiatives.

Measuring the success of CSR initiatives is essential for demonstrating their value and ensuring continuous improvement. Organizations must establish clear metrics and key performance indicators, regularly monitor and evaluate their activities, and transparently report their findings using recognized frameworks and standards. This process ensures accountability and builds trust with stakeholders, showcasing the organization's commitment to making a positive impact.

By integrating social responsibility into their core operations, companies can create a positive impact on society and the environment while enhancing their own sustainability and success. The insights and strategies discussed in this chapter provide a comprehensive guide for developing, implementing, and measuring effective CSR initiatives. Let these principles inspire you to deepen your organization's commitment to CSR. By embracing CSR as a strategic imperative, you can foster a culture of responsibility, drive meaningful change, and build stronger relationships with stakeholders. Ultimately, this commitment will not only benefit society and the environment but also contribute to the long-term success and resilience of your organization. Embrace the challenge of making a positive impact and lead your organization towards a future where business and social good are inextricably linked.

Chapter 13: Social Justice, Diversity, and Inclusion

In the modern workplace, fostering a culture of social justice, diversity, and inclusion is not only a moral imperative but also a strategic advantage. Chapter 13 delves into the critical importance of these principles in shaping a fair, innovative, and high-performing organization. As the global workforce becomes increasingly diverse, organizations must actively promote inclusive practices that respect and leverage the unique perspectives and talents of all employees. This chapter explores how to create an inclusive hiring process, promote diversity and inclusion in the workplace, implement strategies for social justice in organizational policies, and accommodate diverse needs through flexible work arrangements.

Creating an inclusive hiring process is the first step towards building a diverse workforce. This involves attracting talent from a wide range of backgrounds and ensuring that recruitment practices are free from bias. By broadening the talent pool and implementing fair evaluation criteria, organizations can hire individuals who bring varied experiences and viewpoints, driving creativity and innovation.

Promoting diversity and inclusion in the workplace goes beyond hiring. It requires an ongoing commitment to creating an environment where all employees feel valued and empowered to contribute their best work. This includes implementing bias training, establishing Employee Resource Groups (ERGs), and developing mentorship programs. Regular diversity audits help organizations assess their progress and identify areas for improvement, ensuring that inclusion remains a priority.

Strategies for social justice in organizational policies are essential for addressing systemic inequalities and promoting fairness.

Integrating social justice principles into the company's mission and values guides decision-making and behavior across the organization. Ensuring equitable compensation practices, creating transparent grievance mechanisms, and engaging with communities and stakeholders are key components of this approach. By partnering with social justice organizations and providing ongoing education on these issues, companies can demonstrate their commitment to fostering a just and equitable workplace.

Promoting flexible work arrangements is another crucial aspect of supporting a diverse workforce. Flexible schedules, remote work options, and other accommodations help employees balance their professional and personal lives, catering to different needs and lifestyles. This flexibility not only enhances employee satisfaction and retention but also attracts a broader range of talent.

As we explore these topics, Chapter 13 will provide practical insights and strategies for embedding social justice, diversity, and inclusion into the organizational culture. By embracing these principles, organizations can create a more equitable, innovative, and resilient workforce, ultimately driving long-term success and sustainability. Let this chapter inspire you to take concrete steps towards fostering a workplace where everyone can thrive and contribute to their fullest potential.

Developing an inclusive hiring process is essential for building a workforce that reflects diverse backgrounds and perspectives. This approach not only enhances creativity and innovation but also ensures that the organization benefits from a wide range of experiences and viewpoints. To create an inclusive hiring process, organizations must adopt strategies that attract, assess, and select candidates in a manner free from bias and discrimination.

The first step in creating an inclusive hiring process is to broaden the talent pool. This involves reaching out to diverse communities and using a variety of channels to advertise job openings. Utilizing platforms that cater to underrepresented groups and attending job fairs that focus on diversity can help attract a wide array of candidates. Additionally, crafting inclusive job descriptions that use gender-neutral language and emphasize the organization's commitment to diversity can make positions more appealing to a broader audience.

Implementing blind recruitment techniques can further reduce bias in the hiring process. This method involves removing personal information, such as names, gender, and age, from applications to ensure that candidates are evaluated solely on their qualifications and experience. Blind recruitment helps focus on the candidate's skills and potential rather than any unconscious biases that might influence decision-making.

Structured interviews are another effective tool for promoting inclusivity in hiring. By using a standardized set of questions for all candidates, organizations can ensure that each applicant is evaluated based on the same criteria. This consistency helps reduce the impact of individual biases and allows for a more objective comparison of candidates. Additionally, involving a diverse panel of interviewers can provide multiple perspectives and further mitigate the influence of bias.

Training hiring managers and recruitment teams on unconscious bias is crucial for fostering an inclusive hiring process. These training sessions can raise awareness about the different types of biases that may affect hiring decisions and provide strategies for mitigating their impact. By understanding how unconscious bias operates, hiring professionals can take proactive steps to ensure a fairer evaluation of all candidates.

Developing partnerships with educational institutions, professional associations, and community organizations that serve underrepresented groups can also enhance the inclusivity of the hiring process. These partnerships can help organizations connect with a diverse pool of candidates and create pipelines for future talent. Offering internships, scholarships, and mentorship programs to individuals from diverse backgrounds can further support these efforts and build long-term relationships.

Ensuring transparency throughout the hiring process is another key element. Clearly communicating the stages of the hiring process, the criteria for selection, and the expected timelines helps build trust with candidates. Providing feedback to applicants, whether they are successful or not, can also demonstrate the organization's commitment to fairness and continuous improvement.

Regularly reviewing and analyzing hiring data is essential for maintaining an inclusive hiring process. Organizations should track metrics such as the diversity of applicant pools, the progression of candidates through different stages, and the diversity of hires. This data can identify potential barriers or biases in the hiring process and inform necessary adjustments to promote greater inclusivity.

Creating an inclusive hiring process involves broadening the talent pool, implementing blind recruitment techniques, using structured interviews, training hiring teams on unconscious bias, developing partnerships with diverse organizations, ensuring transparency, and regularly reviewing hiring data. By adopting these strategies, organizations can attract and select talent from diverse backgrounds, fostering a more innovative and dynamic workforce that drives success and growth.

Promoting diversity and inclusion in the workplace requires a continuous and concerted effort to create an environment where all employees feel valued and empowered. This begins with leadership commitment to diversity and inclusion, where leaders model inclusive behaviors and set clear expectations for the entire organization. Implementing bias training for all employees raises awareness of unconscious biases and provides strategies to mitigate their impact. Creating Employee Resource Groups (ERGs) supports underrepresented groups by fostering a sense of community and belonging, and these groups can also provide valuable insights into the needs and experiences of diverse employees.

Mentorship and sponsorship programs play a crucial role in promoting diversity and inclusion. By pairing employees with mentors or sponsors, organizations can help individuals from diverse backgrounds advance in their careers and achieve leadership positions. These programs not only support individual development but also contribute to a more diverse leadership pipeline.

Conducting regular diversity audits allows organizations to assess their current state of diversity and inclusion, identify areas for improvement, and measure progress over time. These audits can inform the development of targeted initiatives to address specific gaps or challenges.

Promoting flexible work arrangements is another critical aspect of fostering an inclusive workplace. Flexible schedules, remote work options, and other accommodations help employees balance their professional and personal lives, catering to different needs and lifestyles. This flexibility not only enhances employee satisfaction and retention but also attracts a broader range of talent.

Communication and education are vital components of promoting diversity and inclusion. Organizations should ensure that diversity and inclusion are integral parts of their internal and external communications, highlighting their commitment to these values. Providing ongoing education on diversity, equity, and inclusion helps keep these issues at the forefront of employees' minds and encourages continuous learning and growth.

Celebrating cultural differences and milestones can also enhance inclusion. Recognizing and celebrating various cultural events and holidays demonstrates respect for diversity and helps build a more inclusive environment. These celebrations can provide opportunities for employees to share their cultural backgrounds and learn from one another.

Promoting diversity and inclusion in the workplace involves leadership commitment, bias training, support through Employee Resource Groups, mentorship and sponsorship programs, diversity audits, flexible work arrangements, effective communication, continuous education, and celebrating cultural differences. By embedding these practices into the organizational culture, companies can create a more inclusive, innovative, and dynamic work environment that drives success and growth.

Integrating social justice into organizational policies involves embedding principles of fairness, equity, and inclusion into every aspect of the company's operations. This process begins with incorporating social justice into the company's mission, vision, and values, ensuring these principles guide all decision-making and behavior. Ensuring equitable compensation practices is crucial, which includes conducting regular pay equity analyses to identify and address any disparities that may exist within the organization.

Creating transparent and accessible grievance mechanisms is essential for addressing instances of discrimination, harassment, and inequality. These mechanisms should be designed to protect confidentiality and provide clear, fair processes for resolving complaints. Engaging with communities and stakeholders is another key strategy. By understanding their needs and perspectives, organizations can incorporate this feedback into their policies and practices, making them more inclusive and effective.

Partnering with social justice organizations and initiatives can demonstrate a company's commitment to broader societal change. These partnerships provide additional resources and expertise, helping organizations to implement effective social justice strategies and amplify their impact. Regularly providing training and education on social justice issues keeps employees informed and engaged with ongoing efforts to promote equity and inclusion. This continuous education fosters a deeper understanding of social justice and encourages employees to actively participate in creating a fairer workplace.

Implementing policies that promote diversity and inclusion in hiring, promotion, and daily operations is fundamental. These policies should aim to remove barriers to entry and advancement for underrepresented groups and create a supportive environment for all employees. Regularly reviewing and updating these policies ensures they remain relevant and effective in addressing the evolving challenges of social justice.

Ensuring social justice in organizational policies involves integrating equity and inclusion into the company's core values, implementing equitable compensation practices, creating transparent grievance mechanisms, engaging with stakeholders, partnering with social justice organizations, providing continuous education, and regularly reviewing policies. By adopting these strategies, organizations can build a fairer, more inclusive workplace that supports long-term success and sustainability.

Promoting flexible work arrangements is essential for accommodating the diverse needs and lifestyles of a modern workforce. Flexible work options, such as remote work, flexible hours, and compressed workweeks, allow employees to balance their professional and personal lives more effectively. This flexibility helps to attract and retain talent from a wide range of backgrounds, including those who might otherwise face barriers to traditional work schedules, such as parents, caregivers, and individuals with disabilities.

Implementing flexible work arrangements involves creating policies that support various work styles and preferences. These policies should be clearly communicated to all employees, ensuring that everyone understands their options and the guidelines for using them. Providing the necessary tools and technologies is also crucial. Access to reliable internet, collaboration software, and secure data systems enables employees to work efficiently from any location.

Leadership support is vital for the success of flexible work arrangements. Leaders must model flexible work behaviors and encourage their teams to take advantage of these options. This support helps to normalize flexible work and reduce any stigma associated with non-traditional work arrangements. Regularly soliciting feedback from employees about their experiences with flexible work can help organizations identify areas for improvement and ensure that the policies meet the evolving needs of the workforce.

Training and development opportunities should be accessible to all employees, regardless of their work arrangements. Offering online courses, virtual workshops, and remote mentoring ensures that employees who work flexibly can continue to grow and advance in their careers. This commitment to professional development supports employee engagement and retention.

Creating a culture of trust and accountability is essential for managing flexible work arrangements effectively. Setting clear expectations for performance and outcomes allows employees to understand their responsibilities and how their work will be evaluated. Regular check-ins and performance reviews help maintain open communication and ensure that employees stay aligned with organizational goals.

Promoting flexible work arrangements involves developing supportive policies, providing necessary tools, ensuring leadership support, offering accessible training and development, and fostering a culture of trust and accountability. By accommodating different needs and lifestyles, organizations can create a more inclusive and diverse workforce that is engaged, productive, and committed to the company's success.

Chapter 13 has explored the critical importance of social justice, diversity, and inclusion in the workplace, highlighting practical strategies for fostering a more equitable and inclusive organizational culture. By promoting these principles, organizations not only fulfill their ethical responsibilities but also drive innovation, enhance employee engagement, and achieve sustainable success.

We began by discussing the creation of an inclusive hiring process to attract diverse talent from different backgrounds and perspectives. This involves broadening the talent pool, implementing unbiased recruitment techniques, and ensuring transparency and fairness throughout the hiring process. By doing so, organizations can build a diverse workforce that brings a variety of experiences and viewpoints, fostering creativity and innovation.

Promoting diversity and inclusion in the workplace requires ongoing efforts to create an environment where all employees feel valued and empowered. Leadership commitment, bias training, Employee Resource Groups, mentorship programs, and regular diversity audits are key components of this strategy. Additionally, promoting flexible work arrangements helps accommodate different needs and lifestyles, further supporting a diverse workforce.

Strategies for social justice in organizational policies are essential for addressing systemic inequalities and ensuring fairness. Integrating social justice principles into the company's mission and values, ensuring equitable compensation practices, creating transparent grievance mechanisms, and engaging with communities and stakeholders are crucial steps. Partnering with social justice organizations and providing continuous education on these issues demonstrate the company's commitment to fostering a just and equitable workplace.

Promoting flexible work arrangements is another critical aspect of supporting a diverse workforce. By offering remote work options, flexible hours, and other accommodations, organizations can help employees balance their professional and personal lives. This flexibility not only enhances employee satisfaction and retention but also attracts a broader range of talent.

As we conclude Chapter 13, it is evident that promoting social justice, diversity, and inclusion is not just a moral imperative but a strategic advantage. By embedding these principles into the organizational culture, companies can create a more equitable, innovative, and dynamic work environment. This commitment to diversity and inclusion drives long-term success and sustainability, positioning the organization as a leader in its industry.

Moving forward, let the insights and strategies discussed in this chapter inspire you to take concrete steps towards fostering a workplace where everyone can thrive. By embracing social justice, diversity, and inclusion, you can build a resilient and high-performing organization that is well-equipped to meet the challenges and opportunities of the modern business landscape. Through these efforts, you will not only enhance the well-being of your employees but also contribute positively to society, creating a better future for all.

Chapter 14: Transformational Leadership Methods

In an era of rapid change and increasing complexity, transformational leadership has emerged as a critical approach for guiding organizations through uncertainty and driving significant positive change. Chapter 14 delves into the methods and principles of transformational leadership, exploring how leaders can inspire and motivate their teams to achieve exceptional results. This chapter will examine the key characteristics of transformational leaders, strategies for developing transformational leadership skills, and the profound impact these leaders have on both organizational change and employee engagement.

Transformational leadership is characterized by the ability to inspire and empower others to achieve their fullest potential and exceed their own expectations. These leaders are visionary, charismatic, and highly effective at fostering a sense of purpose and commitment among their followers. By articulating a clear and compelling vision for the future, transformational leaders can rally their teams around shared goals and drive collective efforts towards achieving them.

Developing transformational leadership skills involves a combination of self-awareness, continuous learning, and practical experience. Leaders must cultivate a deep understanding of their strengths and weaknesses, seek out opportunities for personal and professional growth, and apply their insights in real-world situations. This development process often includes training programs, mentorship, and feedback mechanisms that help leaders refine their abilities and expand their impact.

The impact of transformational leadership on organizational change is profound. Transformational leaders are adept at identifying opportunities for innovation, driving strategic initiatives, and navigating complex challenges. Their ability to communicate a compelling vision and foster a culture of trust and collaboration enables organizations to adapt to changing environments, seize new opportunities, and achieve sustainable growth. By promoting a culture of continuous improvement and resilience, transformational leaders ensure that their organizations remain competitive and future-ready.

The influence of transformational leadership extends beyond organizational change to significantly impact employees. These leaders foster a supportive and empowering work environment where employees feel valued, motivated, and engaged. By providing individualized support, recognizing achievements, and encouraging professional development, transformational leaders help employees realize their potential and contribute meaningfully to the organization. This approach not only enhances job satisfaction and retention but also drives higher levels of performance and innovation.

As we explore the characteristics and methods of transformational leadership, this chapter will provide practical insights and strategies for cultivating these essential leadership qualities. By embracing transformational leadership, you can inspire your team, drive organizational change, and create a thriving work environment that supports both individual and collective success. Let this chapter guide you in developing the skills and mindset needed to lead with vision, empathy, and effectiveness, ultimately transforming your organization and its people.

Transformational leaders are defined by their ability to inspire and motivate others to achieve their fullest potential. They possess a clear and compelling vision for the future, which they effectively communicate to their teams, creating a shared sense of purpose and direction. Their charismatic nature enables them to build strong, trusting relationships, fostering a positive and collaborative work environment. They demonstrate a high level of emotional intelligence, showing empathy and understanding towards their employees' needs and concerns.

These leaders are also known for their commitment to continuous improvement and innovation. They challenge the status quo and encourage their teams to think creatively and embrace new ideas. By promoting a culture of learning and growth, transformational leaders help their organizations adapt to changing environments and stay competitive. Their ability to provide individualized support and mentorship helps employees develop their skills and advance in their careers.

Transformational leaders are also highly effective at recognizing and leveraging the strengths of their team members. They empower employees by delegating responsibilities and giving them the autonomy to make decisions. This approach not only boosts morale and job satisfaction but also enhances overall team performance. Additionally, they are adept at managing change, guiding their organizations through transitions with confidence and clarity.

Their ethical and moral integrity is another defining characteristic. Transformational leaders lead by example, demonstrating a commitment to ethical behavior and decision-making. This integrity builds trust and respect among their teams, reinforcing the leader's credibility and authority. They are also adept at fostering a sense of community and belonging within the organization, ensuring that every team member feels valued and included.

The ability to inspire and motivate, clear vision, emotional intelligence, commitment to innovation, individual support, empowerment, change management, ethical integrity, and fostering a sense of community are the core characteristics of transformational leaders. These qualities enable them to drive significant positive change within their organizations and create a supportive and dynamic work environment where employees can thrive.

Developing transformational leadership skills requires a blend of self-awareness, continuous learning, and practical application. Self-awareness is the foundation, as leaders must understand their strengths and weaknesses to effectively inspire and guide others. This can be achieved through reflective practices, feedback from colleagues, and formal assessments. Continuous learning is essential, involving the pursuit of knowledge through reading, attending workshops, and engaging in professional development programs focused on leadership and management.

Practical application of these skills is equally important. Leaders should seek opportunities to apply their learning in real-world situations, which helps to reinforce new skills and refine existing ones. This can involve taking on challenging projects, leading cross-functional teams, or volunteering for leadership roles in professional organizations. These experiences provide valuable insights and help leaders develop resilience and adaptability.

Mentorship and coaching are also crucial components of developing transformational leadership skills. Engaging with a mentor or coach provides guidance, support, and perspective from someone with more experience. This relationship can help leaders navigate complex situations, build confidence, and accelerate their development. Additionally, mentoring others can enhance a leader's skills, as teaching and guiding employees require clarity and empathy.

Emotional intelligence is a key attribute of transformational leaders and can be developed through intentional practice. This involves improving self-regulation, empathy, and social skills by actively seeking to understand and manage one's own emotions and those of others. Techniques such as mindfulness, active listening, and conflict resolution training can enhance emotional intelligence.

Building a strong vision and effectively communicating it is another vital skill. Leaders should practice articulating their vision clearly and persuasively, ensuring it aligns with the organization's goals and values. This can involve storytelling techniques, public speaking, and consistent messaging across various platforms.

Creating a culture of continuous improvement and innovation is essential. Leaders can foster this culture by encouraging experimentation, supporting risk-taking, and rewarding creative solutions. Providing resources for professional development and creating an environment where employees feel safe to express new ideas can stimulate ongoing growth and innovation.

Ethical integrity must be at the core of transformational leadership. Leaders should consistently demonstrate ethical behavior, make decisions based on core values, and foster an environment of transparency and trust. This integrity not only builds respect but also sets a standard for the entire organization.

Developing transformational leadership skills involves cultivating self-awareness, engaging in continuous learning, applying skills in practical settings, seeking mentorship, enhancing emotional intelligence, articulating a strong vision, fostering a culture of innovation, and upholding ethical integrity. These efforts collectively enable leaders to inspire and motivate their teams, drive positive change, and build a resilient, dynamic organization.

Transformational leadership profoundly impacts organizational change by fostering an environment conducive to innovation, adaptability, and continuous improvement. Leaders with transformational qualities effectively communicate a compelling vision for the future, which aligns with the organization's strategic goals and inspires employees to commit to the change process. Their ability to articulate this vision clearly and persuasively ensures that everyone understands the purpose and benefits of the proposed changes, creating a unified effort towards achieving these objectives.

These leaders excel in identifying opportunities for innovation and driving strategic initiatives. They challenge the status quo, encouraging their teams to think creatively and explore new solutions. This openness to new ideas helps organizations stay competitive in rapidly changing markets and adapt to emerging trends. By promoting a culture of trust and collaboration, transformational leaders facilitate seamless teamwork and cross-functional cooperation, which are essential for successful change implementation.

Transformational leaders also excel in navigating complex challenges that arise during the change process. Their resilience and adaptability enable them to guide their organizations through uncertainty with confidence and clarity. They provide the necessary support and resources to their teams, ensuring that employees feel equipped and empowered to embrace new ways of working. This support includes offering training and development opportunities that help employees acquire the skills needed to succeed in the changing environment.

The ethical integrity and emotional intelligence of transformational leaders further enhance their impact on organizational change. By leading with integrity, they build trust and credibility, which are crucial for gaining buy-in from employees and other stakeholders. Their ability to understand and manage emotions helps them address resistance to change effectively, fostering a positive and supportive atmosphere.

Transformational leadership drives organizational change by inspiring a shared vision, promoting innovation, fostering collaboration, providing support and resources, and leading with integrity and emotional intelligence. These leaders create an environment where change is not only accepted but embraced, enabling organizations to navigate challenges and seize new opportunities for growth and success. This kind of leadership significantly impacts employees by fostering a work environment where they feel valued, motivated, and engaged. Leaders who exhibit transformational qualities inspire their teams with a compelling vision and a sense of purpose, helping employees see how their individual contributions align with the broader organizational goals. This alignment enhances job satisfaction and instills a sense of pride and ownership in their work.

By providing individualized support and recognizing the unique strengths and needs of each employee, transformational leaders create a supportive and nurturing environment. They offer mentorship, guidance, and opportunities for professional development, enabling employees to grow and advance in their careers. This personalized approach boosts morale and encourages a continuous pursuit of excellence.

Transformational leaders also foster a culture of open communication and trust. They actively listen to employees' ideas, concerns, and feedback, creating a space where everyone feels heard and valued. This inclusivity promotes a sense of belonging and reduces feelings of isolation or alienation, particularly in diverse and remote teams. Employees are more likely to share their innovative ideas and collaborate effectively when they feel respected and supported.

Emotional intelligence is a hallmark of transformational leaders, allowing them to connect with employees on a deeper level. By demonstrating empathy and understanding, they build strong, trusting relationships that enhance team cohesion and cooperation. This emotional connection helps employees feel more comfortable taking risks and trying new approaches, knowing they have the support of their leader.

The recognition and rewards provided by transformational leaders for employees' hard work and achievements further boost motivation and engagement. Regular acknowledgment of contributions, whether through formal awards or simple expressions of gratitude, reinforces positive behaviors and encourages continued high performance. This recognition fosters a positive work environment where employees are motivated to excel and contribute their best efforts.

Transformational leaders also encourage a culture of innovation and continuous improvement. By challenging the status quo and supporting creative problem-solving, they empower employees to think outside the box and pursue new ideas. This empowerment not only drives individual growth but also contributes to the organization's overall success by fostering a culture of agility and adaptability.

Transformational leadership positively impacts employees by aligning their efforts with organizational goals, providing personalized support and development opportunities, fostering open communication and trust, building strong emotional connections, recognizing and rewarding contributions, and encouraging innovation. These factors collectively create a dynamic and supportive work environment where employees feel motivated, engaged, and empowered to achieve their full potential.

Chapter 14 has explored the transformative power of leadership that inspires, motivates, and drives significant positive change within organizations. By exploring the characteristics of transformational leaders, strategies for developing these essential leadership skills, and their profound impact on both organizational change and employee engagement, we have highlighted how this leadership approach is pivotal in navigating the complexities of the modern business environment.

Transformational leaders are visionary, charismatic, emotionally intelligent, and ethically grounded individuals who inspire their teams through a compelling vision and a strong sense of purpose. They foster a culture of continuous improvement and innovation, challenge the status quo, and empower employees to reach their full potential. By providing individualized support and promoting open communication and trust, they create an inclusive and dynamic work environment that encourages creativity and collaboration.

Developing transformational leadership skills involves a combination of self-awareness, continuous learning, and practical application. Leaders must seek opportunities to refine their abilities through training, mentorship, and real-world experiences. Building emotional intelligence, articulating a clear vision, fostering a culture of innovation, and upholding ethical integrity are all critical components of this development process.

The impact of transformational leadership on organizational change is profound. These leaders drive strategic initiatives, promote innovation, and navigate complex challenges with resilience and clarity. Their ability to foster a culture of trust and collaboration ensures that change is embraced and effectively implemented, positioning the organization for long-term success.

Transformational leadership also has a significant impact on employees. By aligning individual contributions with organizational goals, providing personalized support and development opportunities, and fostering a positive work environment, transformational leaders enhance job satisfaction, motivation, and engagement. Their ability to connect with employees on an emotional level builds strong relationships and promotes a sense of belonging and inclusion.

As we conclude Chapter 14, it is clear that embracing transformational leadership methods can profoundly enhance organizational performance and employee well-being. By developing these leadership qualities and applying them effectively, you can inspire your team, drive meaningful change, and create a thriving, resilient organization. Let the insights and strategies discussed in this chapter guide you in becoming a transformational leader who not only achieves exceptional results but also makes a lasting positive impact on your organization and its people.

Moving forward, embrace the challenge of transformational leadership. Inspire your team with a compelling vision, foster a culture of innovation and trust, and lead with empathy and integrity. By doing so, you will not only drive your organization towards success but also create a work environment where everyone can thrive and contribute to their fullest potential.

Part IV: Innovative Methods and Future Directions

As organizations continue to evolve in an ever-changing landscape, the need for innovative methods and forward-thinking strategies becomes increasingly critical. Part IV of this book, "Innovative Methods and Future Directions," explores cutting-edge approaches and emerging trends that are shaping the future of organizational development. This section delves into advanced methodologies such as systems dynamics, appreciative inquiry, dialogic inquiry, and action research, offering a glimpse into how these tools can drive adaptive and resilient organizational designs. It concludes with a reflection on future trends, summarizing key concepts and practices that will guide organizations toward sustainability and long-term success.

Chapter 15: Systems Dynamics and Organizational Design

In this chapter, we explore the principles of systems dynamics and their application in organizational design. Systems dynamics provides a framework for understanding the complex and interconnected nature of organizational processes. By applying these principles, organizations can design structures that are both adaptive and resilient, capable of responding effectively to internal and external changes. We will discuss techniques for mapping organizational systems, identifying feedback loops, and leveraging leverage points to drive significant improvements.

Chapter 16: Appreciative Intelligence and Inquiry

Appreciative inquiry is a powerful approach to organizational development that focuses on identifying and amplifying an organization's strengths. This chapter introduces the concept of appreciative inquiry and its applications in fostering a positive organizational culture. By engaging in appreciative inquiry, organizations can build on what works well, creating a foundation for sustainable growth and development. We will explore practical examples of how appreciative inquiry has been used to drive innovation, enhance collaboration, and improve overall organizational health.

Chapter 17: Dialogic Inquiry and Action Research

Dialogic inquiry and action research are methodologies that emphasize collaborative learning and participatory action. This chapter delves into techniques for conducting dialogic inquiry, which involves open and reflective dialogue among stakeholders to explore complex issues. Action research, on the other hand, combines theory and practice to address real-world problems through iterative cycles of planning, action, and reflection. We will examine how these methods can be effectively applied in organizational settings to foster continuous improvement and adaptive change.

Chapter 18: Concluding Perspectives on Organizational Development

The final chapter of this book offers a reflection on the future trends in organizational development. We will summarize the key concepts and practices discussed throughout the book, highlighting their relevance in the context of emerging challenges and opportunities. This chapter provides a forward-looking perspective on how organizations can build adaptive and sustainable structures that not only survive but thrive in the face of change. We will also reflect on the importance of continuous learning and innovation as foundational elements of successful organizational development.

Part IV of this book equips readers with innovative methods and strategic insights essential for navigating the future of organizational development. By embracing systems dynamics, appreciative inquiry, dialogic inquiry, and action research, organizations can cultivate adaptive and resilient cultures. As we look to the future, the principles and practices outlined in this section will serve as a guide for building organizations that are not only effective and efficient but also inclusive, sustainable, and prepared for the complexities of the modern world.

Chapter 15: Systems Dynamics and Organizational Design

Understanding the interplay between systems dynamics and organizational design is crucial for building adaptive and resilient organizations. Chapter 15 explores how the principles of systems dynamics can be applied to organizational design, providing a comprehensive framework for creating structures that are capable of thriving in both stable and turbulent conditions. By examining the fundamental concepts of systems dynamics and the essential building blocks of organizational design, this chapter offers insights into redesigning modern organizations to meet the demands of postmodern and hypermodern workplaces.

Systems dynamics is a field that studies the behavior of complex systems over time. It focuses on the interrelationships between different components within a system and how these interactions influence overall performance and outcomes. In the context of organizational design, systems dynamics provides valuable tools and methodologies for analyzing and understanding the dynamic nature of organizations. By recognizing patterns, feedback loops, and cause-and-effect relationships, leaders can make more informed decisions that enhance organizational effectiveness and adaptability.

Organizational design involves the arrangement of structures, processes, and resources to achieve organizational goals. The basic building blocks of organizational design include hierarchies, networks, roles, and workflows. Effective organizational design aligns these elements with the organization's strategy, culture, and environment, ensuring that all parts of the organization work together harmoniously to achieve common objectives. Understanding these building blocks is essential for creating organizations that are not only efficient but also flexible and responsive to change.

The transition from modern to postmodern and hypermodern workplaces requires a reevaluation of traditional organizational structures and practices. Postmodern organizations emphasize decentralization, diversity, and collaboration, moving away from rigid hierarchies and embracing more fluid and adaptable forms of organization. Hypermodern workplaces take this a step further, integrating advanced technologies, continuous innovation, and a high degree of agility to stay ahead in an ever-evolving market landscape. Redesigning organizations to fit these paradigms involves adopting new approaches to leadership, communication, and decision-making that support a more dynamic and inclusive organizational culture.

Designing adaptive and resilient organizations is a key objective in applying systems dynamics and modern organizational design principles. Adaptive organizations can respond swiftly to external changes and uncertainties, continuously evolving to meet new challenges and opportunities. Resilient organizations, on the other hand, are robust and capable of withstanding shocks and disruptions while maintaining core functions. Combining these two qualities creates organizations that not only survive but thrive in volatile environments. This requires a focus on continuous learning, innovation, and the ability to pivot strategically when necessary.

As we explore the principles of systems dynamics and the foundational concepts of organizational design, this chapter will provide practical insights and strategies for creating adaptive and resilient organizations. By understanding and applying these principles, leaders can design organizations that are better equipped to navigate the complexities of the modern business world and achieve sustained success. Let this chapter guide you in rethinking and reshaping your organization to meet the demands of todays and tomorrow's dynamic environments.

Systems dynamics is a methodology used to understand the behavior of complex systems over time. It emphasizes the interconnectedness of different components within a system and how their interactions shape the overall performance and outcomes. At its core, systems dynamics relies on the concept of feedback loops, which can be either reinforcing or balancing. Reinforcing feedback loops amplify changes, leading to exponential growth or decline, while balancing feedback loops counteract changes, promoting stability and equilibrium.

A fundamental principle of systems dynamics is the recognition that systems are more than the sum of their parts. The relationships and interactions between elements are as important as the elements themselves. This holistic perspective helps identify leverage points where small changes can produce significant improvements.

Time delays are another critical aspect of systems dynamics. Delays between actions and their effects can complicate decision-making and lead to unintended consequences. Understanding these delays allows for more effective planning and intervention.

Nonlinearity is inherent in complex systems, meaning that changes do not always produce proportional responses. Small inputs can lead to large impacts, and vice versa. This principle highlights the importance of considering a wide range of possible outcomes when analyzing system behavior.

Causality in systems dynamics is often circular rather than linear. This means that cause-and-effect relationships form loops rather than straight lines, creating feedback loops that drive system behavior. Identifying these loops is crucial for understanding the dynamics of the system and predicting its future behavior.

Modeling is a key tool in systems dynamics, allowing for the simulation of different scenarios and the exploration of potential outcomes. These models help visualize the structure and behavior of systems, making it easier to identify leverage points and test interventions.

The principle of system boundaries emphasizes that every system is part of a larger system and contains smaller subsystems. Defining the boundaries of a system is essential for focusing analysis and understanding the context within which the system operates.

Systems dynamics also stresses the importance of mental models, which are the internal representations that individuals use to interpret and interact with the world. These models influence how people perceive and respond to system behavior. By making these mental models explicit, systems dynamics helps improve understanding and decision-making.

The principles of systems dynamics offer a framework for analyzing and managing complex systems. By focusing on feedback loops, time delays, nonlinearity, causality, modeling, system boundaries, and mental models, leaders can better understand the dynamics at play and design more effective interventions. This holistic and analytical approach is essential for navigating the complexities of modern organizational environments and achieving sustainable success.

Organizational design involves arranging structures, processes, and resources to achieve organizational goals effectively. The foundation of organizational design includes several key elements, such as hierarchies, networks, roles, and workflows. Hierarchies establish the levels of authority and responsibility within an organization, determining how decisions are made and how information flows. They provide a clear structure for accountability and oversight but can sometimes lead to rigidity and slow decision-making.

Networks represent the informal and formal relationships between individuals and groups within the organization. These networks facilitate communication, collaboration, and the sharing of knowledge across different parts of the organization. Effective network design ensures that information and resources are accessible to those who need them, promoting innovation and agility.

Roles define the specific responsibilities and expectations for individuals within the organization. Clear role definitions help ensure that everyone understands their duties and how they contribute to the overall mission. Well-defined roles also reduce overlaps and gaps in responsibilities, enhancing efficiency and coordination.

Workflows describe the processes and procedures for completing tasks and achieving objectives. Streamlined workflows ensure that activities are performed efficiently and consistently, reducing waste and improving productivity. Effective workflow design involves mapping out processes, identifying bottlenecks, and implementing improvements to optimize performance.

Aligning these building blocks with the organization's strategy, culture, and environment is essential for effective organizational design. The design must support the strategic objectives of the organization, enabling it to respond to external opportunities and threats. It should also reflect and reinforce the organization's values and norms, fostering a positive and cohesive culture.

Adaptability is a crucial consideration in organizational design. As environments change, organizations must be able to pivot and reconfigure their structures and processes to remain competitive. This requires a flexible design that can accommodate new strategies, technologies, and market conditions.

Innovation is another key factor in organizational design. Structures and processes should encourage creativity and experimentation, allowing the organization to develop new products, services, and ways of working. This involves creating spaces for collaboration, supporting risk-taking, and providing the resources needed for innovation.

Employee engagement and empowerment are also important. Designing an organization that values and leverages the contributions of its people leads to higher motivation and better performance. This can be achieved through participative decision-making, opportunities for professional growth, and recognition of achievements.

Organizational design involves structuring hierarchies, networks, roles, and workflows to achieve strategic goals while fostering a positive culture, adaptability, innovation, and employee engagement. By carefully aligning these elements, organizations can create efficient, flexible, and dynamic environments that support long-term success and resilience.

Redesigning modern organizations to fit postmodern and hypermodern workplaces involves shifting from traditional, hierarchical structures to more flexible, decentralized, and technology-driven models. Postmodern workplaces emphasize decentralization, diversity, and collaboration. These organizations move away from rigid hierarchies and embrace more fluid and adaptive forms of organization, where decision-making is distributed across various levels and teams are empowered to operate with greater autonomy. This approach fosters a more inclusive environment, allowing for a wide range of perspectives and encouraging innovative thinking.

In postmodern organizations, diversity is not only accepted but actively sought out and leveraged as a source of strength. These workplaces prioritize creating a culture that values different backgrounds, experiences, and viewpoints, recognizing that such diversity drives creativity and problem-solving. Collaboration is central to the postmodern organizational model, with cross-functional teams working together on projects and initiatives. This collaborative approach breaks down silos and encourages the sharing of knowledge and resources across the organization.

Hypermodern workplaces take these principles further by integrating advanced technologies and embracing continuous innovation. These organizations are characterized by their agility and ability to rapidly respond to changes in the market. Hypermodern organizations leverage cutting-edge technologies such as artificial intelligence, automation, and data analytics to enhance efficiency, decision-making, and customer engagement.

The use of digital platforms and tools facilitates real-time communication and collaboration, enabling teams to work seamlessly regardless of their physical location.

To redesign an organization for a hypermodern workplace, it is essential to create a culture that embraces change and fosters a mindset of continuous improvement. This involves encouraging employees to experiment, take risks, and learn from failures. Leadership in hypermodern organizations is less about command and control and more about guiding, mentoring, and supporting teams as they navigate complex and dynamic environments.

Flexibility and adaptability are crucial in both postmodern and hypermodern workplaces. Organizational structures need to be designed to allow for rapid reconfiguration in response to new opportunities or challenges. This might involve creating modular teams that can be assembled and disassembled as needed, or implementing flexible work arrangements that enable employees to work when and where they are most productive.

Communication and transparency are also vital. In these reimagined workplaces, information flows freely and openly, ensuring that all employees have access to the knowledge and insights they need to perform their roles effectively. This transparency builds trust and aligns everyone with the organization's goals and values.

Redesigning modern organizations into postmodern and hypermodern workplaces requires a fundamental shift in how we think about organizational structure, culture, and leadership. By embracing decentralization, diversity, collaboration, advanced technologies, and continuous innovation, organizations can create flexible, adaptive, and dynamic environments that are well-equipped to thrive in today's fast-paced and ever-changing business landscape.

Designing adaptive and resilient organizations involves creating structures and processes that can respond swiftly to changes and withstand disruptions while maintaining core functions. An adaptive organization is characterized by its ability to pivot and innovate in response to new opportunities and challenges. This requires a culture that embraces change and fosters continuous learning and improvement. Encouraging a mindset of experimentation and risk-taking allows employees to explore new ideas and approaches without fear of failure.

To support adaptability, organizations need flexible structures that can be reconfigured as needed. This might involve creating modular teams that can be assembled and disassembled based on current needs or implementing flexible work arrangements that enable employees to work when and where they are most productive. Ensuring that decision-making is distributed throughout the organization empowers teams to act quickly and independently, which is crucial for maintaining agility in dynamic environments.

Resilient organizations, on the other hand, are those that can absorb shocks and disruptions while continuing to operate effectively. Building resilience involves identifying and mitigating potential risks, whether they are related to supply chains, cybersecurity, or market volatility. This requires a proactive approach to risk management, including regular assessments and the development of contingency plans.

A resilient organization also fosters strong relationships and networks, both internally and externally. Internally, this means building a cohesive and supportive culture where employees feel valued and connected. Externally, it involves establishing robust partnerships and collaborations with suppliers, customers, and other stakeholders. These relationships can provide crucial support and resources during times of crisis.

Technology plays a critical role in both adaptability and resilience. Leveraging advanced technologies such as artificial intelligence, automation, and data analytics enhances an organization's ability to anticipate and respond to changes. These tools can provide real-time insights and predictive analytics that inform decision-making and strategy. Additionally, ensuring robust cybersecurity measures protects the organization from digital threats and ensures business continuity.

Leadership is key to fostering adaptability and resilience. Leaders must model the behaviors they wish to see, such as openness to change, a commitment to continuous learning, and a focus on collaboration and inclusivity. Effective leaders also communicate a clear vision and strategy, aligning everyone in the organization around common goals and values. This alignment helps to create a sense of purpose and direction, which is crucial during times of uncertainty.

Employee engagement and empowerment are essential components of adaptive and resilient organizations. By involving employees in decision-making processes and providing opportunities for professional growth, organizations can harness the full potential of their workforce. This engagement not only drives innovation but also strengthens the organization's ability to adapt and thrive.

Designing adaptive and resilient organizations involves creating flexible structures, fostering a culture of continuous learning and improvement, proactive risk management, leveraging advanced technologies, and strong leadership. By focusing on these elements, organizations can build the capacity to respond to change and withstand disruptions, ensuring long-term success and sustainability.

Chapter 15 has explored the essential elements of systems dynamics and organizational design, providing a comprehensive framework for creating adaptive and resilient organizations. In today's rapidly changing business environment, understanding and applying these principles are critical for achieving sustained success and competitive advantage.

We began by delving into the principles of systems dynamics, highlighting the importance of feedback loops, time delays, nonlinearity, causality, modeling, system boundaries, and mental models. These principles offer a holistic approach to analyzing and managing complex organizational systems, enabling leaders to identify leverage points and design effective interventions.

We then examined the basic building blocks of organizational design, such as hierarchies, networks, roles, and workflows. Effective organizational design aligns these elements with the organization's strategy, culture, and environment, ensuring that all parts work together harmoniously to achieve common objectives. Adaptability, innovation, and employee engagement are key considerations in this process.

Redesigning modern organizations to fit postmodern and hypermodern workplaces involves moving away from traditional, hierarchical structures towards more flexible, decentralized, and technology-driven models. Postmodern workplaces emphasize decentralization, diversity, and collaboration, while hypermodern workplaces integrate advanced technologies and continuous innovation. This shift requires new approaches to leadership, communication, and decision-making that support a more dynamic and inclusive organizational culture.

Finally, we discussed the principles of designing adaptive and resilient organizations. Adaptive organizations are characterized by their ability to pivot and innovate in response to new opportunities and challenges. Resilient organizations can absorb shocks and disruptions while continuing to operate effectively. Building adaptability and resilience involves fostering a culture of continuous learning and improvement, proactive risk management, leveraging advanced technologies, and strong leadership.

As we conclude Chapter 15, it is evident that designing organizations capable of thriving in today's complex and volatile environment requires a deep understanding of systems dynamics and organizational design. By embracing these principles, leaders can create structures that are not only efficient and effective but also flexible and robust. This approach ensures that organizations are well-equipped to navigate the uncertainties of the modern business landscape and seize new opportunities for growth and innovation.

Let the insights and strategies discussed in this chapter inspire you to rethink and reshape your organization. By applying the principles of systems dynamics and organizational design, you can build an adaptive and resilient organization that excels in both stable and turbulent times. Embrace the challenge of creating a dynamic and inclusive workplace where innovation, collaboration, and continuous improvement are at the forefront, driving your organization towards long-term success and sustainability.

Chapter 16: Appreciative Intelligence and Inquiry

The concepts of Appreciative Intelligence and Appreciative Inquiry have gained significant attention for their transformative potential. Chapter 16 delves into these innovative approaches, exploring how they can be harnessed to foster positive change and drive organizational success. By shifting the focus from problem-solving to recognizing and amplifying strengths, these methodologies offer a fresh perspective on enhancing performance, engagement, and overall well-being within organizations.

Appreciative Intelligence is the ability to perceive the positive inherent potential in a given situation and to act purposefully to transform that potential into outcomes. It involves seeing possibilities, envisioning a better future, and being resilient in the face of challenges. Appreciative Intelligence matters because it empowers individuals and organizations to focus on opportunities rather than obstacles, fostering a proactive and optimistic mindset that drives innovation and growth. Leaders with high Appreciative Intelligence can inspire their teams, cultivate a culture of positivity, and unlock the full potential of their workforce.

The concept of Appreciative Inquiry takes this idea further by providing a structured approach to organizational change. Appreciative Inquiry is a collaborative and strength-based process that engages stakeholders in identifying and amplifying what works well within an organization. Instead of focusing on problems and deficits, Appreciative Inquiry encourages participants to explore their organization's successes, values, and aspirations. This positive framework leads to more sustainable and impactful change by building on the existing strengths and achievements of the organization.

In organizational development, Appreciative Inquiry can be applied in various ways. It is often used in strategic planning, team building, leadership development, and culture change initiatives. By engaging employees in meaningful conversations about their best experiences and hopes for the future, organizations can create a shared vision that motivates and unites everyone. This approach also fosters a sense of ownership and empowerment, as employees are actively involved in shaping the direction of the organization.

Looking to the future, using an appreciative framework opens up numerous possibilities for innovation and growth. Organizations can continue to evolve by consistently applying Appreciative Intelligence and Inquiry to their practices. This might involve incorporating these principles into everyday interactions, decision-making processes, and long-term strategic planning. By maintaining a focus on strengths and opportunities, organizations can remain agile and resilient, capable of navigating an ever-changing business landscape with confidence and creativity.

As we explore the principles and applications of Appreciative Intelligence and Inquiry, this chapter will provide practical insights and strategies for integrating these approaches into your organization. By embracing an appreciative framework, you can foster a culture of positivity, drive meaningful change, and unlock new levels of performance and engagement. Let this chapter guide you in leveraging the power of appreciation to create a thriving, dynamic organization that is well-equipped for future success.

Appreciative Intelligence is the ability to recognize the positive potential within a situation and to envision and act towards realizing that potential. This concept goes beyond mere optimism; it involves a deep-seated ability to see possibilities where others see obstacles, to envision a compelling future, and to persistently work towards that future despite challenges and setbacks. Appreciative Intelligence is rooted in a mindset that focuses on strengths, opportunities, and the inherent value in every situation.

The significance of Appreciative Intelligence lies in its transformative impact on individuals and organizations. Leaders with high Appreciative Intelligence can inspire and motivate their teams by consistently focusing on what is possible rather than what is wrong. This positive orientation fosters a culture of innovation and resilience, where employees feel empowered to explore new ideas and solutions. When leaders highlight potential and celebrate successes, it builds confidence and encourages a proactive approach to challenges.

Appreciative Intelligence matters because it cultivates an environment where positive change is not only possible but expected. In such an environment, setbacks are viewed as opportunities for growth and learning rather than as insurmountable failures. This perspective helps organizations navigate through uncertainty and change with greater agility and creativity. By emphasizing what is working well and building on those strengths, organizations can achieve sustainable growth and continuous improvement. Furthermore, Appreciative Intelligence contributes to higher levels of employee engagement and satisfaction. When employees are encouraged to focus on their strengths and see the positive impact of their work, they are more likely to feel valued and motivated. This leads to increased productivity, better teamwork, and a stronger alignment with the organization's goals and values. In essence, Appreciative Intelligence creates a virtuous cycle where positive thinking and action reinforce each other, driving ongoing success and development.

In the broader context of organizational development, Appreciative Intelligence plays a crucial role in shaping strategies, fostering innovation, and building resilient cultures. It helps organizations to not only survive but thrive in dynamic and competitive environments. By adopting an appreciative mindset, leaders and teams can unlock new possibilities, harness the full potential of their resources, and create a more fulfilling and successful organizational experience.

Appreciative Intelligence is a powerful capability that enables individuals and organizations to recognize and realize positive potential. It matters because it drives innovation, resilience, engagement, and sustainable success, transforming the way we approach challenges and opportunities in the workplace. By cultivating Appreciative Intelligence, leaders can foster a thriving, dynamic, and future-ready organization.

Appreciative Inquiry is a collaborative and strength-based approach to organizational change that focuses on identifying and amplifying what works well within an organization. Rather than concentrating on problems and deficits, Appreciative Inquiry encourages stakeholders to explore their organization's successes, values, and aspirations. This method involves engaging employees in meaningful conversations about their best experiences and envisioning a positive future together.

The process of Appreciative Inquiry typically follows a cycle known as the 4-D model: Discovery, Dream, Design, and Destiny (or Delivery). In the Discovery phase, participants share stories of times when they felt most engaged and proud of their work. These stories help uncover the core strengths and values that drive the organization. During the Dream phase, stakeholders collectively envision an ideal future, building on the strengths identified in the Discovery phase. This visioning process fosters creativity and alignment around shared goals.

In the Design phase, participants develop concrete plans and strategies to achieve the envisioned future. This involves co-creating initiatives and actions that leverage the organization's strengths and resources. Finally, in the Destiny phase, the organization implements the designed strategies, with a focus on continuous learning and adaptation. This phase emphasizes sustaining momentum and ensuring that the positive changes become deeply embedded in the organizational culture.

Appreciative Inquiry is based on the principle that organizations grow in the direction of what they consistently ask questions about and focus on. By framing inquiries in a positive light, it shifts the focus from problems to possibilities, creating an environment that encourages optimism, engagement, and innovation. This positive framework helps build a more inclusive and collaborative organizational culture, where everyone feels valued and empowered to contribute to the collective success.

The impact of Appreciative Inquiry extends beyond individual projects or initiatives. It fosters a culture of continuous improvement and resilience, where strengths and successes are regularly celebrated and built upon. This approach not only enhances organizational performance but also improves employee morale and engagement. By focusing on what works well and envisioning a better future, Appreciative Inquiry helps organizations navigate change more effectively and achieve sustainable growth.

The concept of Appreciative Inquiry represents a shift from problem-solving to recognizing and amplifying strengths. It involves engaging stakeholders in a positive dialogue about their best experiences and aspirations, co-creating a shared vision for the future, and developing concrete plans to achieve that vision. This approach fosters a culture of optimism, collaboration, and continuous improvement, driving meaningful and sustainable organizational change.

Appreciative Inquiry has a wide range of applications in organizational development, offering a positive and collaborative approach to driving change and fostering growth. In strategic planning, Appreciative Inquiry helps organizations identify their core strengths and envision a compelling future. By involving stakeholders in discussions about their best experiences and aspirations, organizations can create strategic plans that are aligned with their values and strengths, ensuring greater buy-in and commitment to the plan's implementation. In team building, Appreciative Inquiry strengthens relationships and enhances collaboration. Teams engage in positive storytelling, sharing moments when they felt most effective and engaged. This process helps build trust, mutual respect, and a deeper understanding of each team member's contributions. By focusing on shared successes, teams can develop a more cohesive and supportive working environment.

Leadership development is another key area where Appreciative Inquiry is highly effective. Leaders are encouraged to reflect on their most impactful moments and identify the qualities that contributed to their success. This reflection fosters self-awareness and helps leaders build on their strengths. Additionally, Appreciative Inquiry can be used to create a vision for leadership that aligns with the organization's values and goals, guiding leaders in their development journey.

In organizational culture change initiatives, Appreciative Inquiry plays a crucial role in shifting the focus from problems to possibilities. By engaging employees in conversations about what they value most in the organization's culture and what they hope to see in the future, Appreciative Inquiry helps create a shared vision for cultural transformation. This positive approach ensures that culture change initiatives are grounded in the organization's strengths and are more likely to be embraced by employees.

Appreciative Inquiry is also effective in conflict resolution and improving workplace relationships. By encouraging individuals to focus on positive interactions and shared goals, it helps reduce tensions and build a more collaborative and harmonious work environment. This approach fosters open communication and empathy, enabling employees to work through conflicts constructively.

In innovation and continuous improvement efforts, Appreciative Inquiry stimulates creative thinking and problem-solving. By focusing on past successes and exploring how these can be expanded or replicated, organizations can identify new opportunities for growth and improvement. This positive orientation encourages experimentation and a willingness to take risks, driving innovation and excellence. Appreciative Inquiry's applications in organizational development are diverse and impactful. It enhances strategic planning, team building, leadership development, culture change, conflict resolution, and innovation efforts. By focusing on strengths and possibilities, Appreciative Inquiry fosters a positive, engaged, and forward-thinking organizational environment that supports sustainable growth and success.

Using an appreciative framework opens up numerous possibilities for the future, particularly in how organizations can evolve and adapt. One idea is to embed Appreciative Inquiry into daily operations, making it a core part of the organizational culture. This involves regularly holding positive-focused meetings where successes are highlighted and strengths are leveraged for future projects. By continually focusing on what works well, organizations can maintain high levels of engagement and innovation.

Incorporating technology into the appreciative framework is another future idea. Digital platforms and tools can facilitate virtual Appreciative Inquiry sessions, allowing for broader participation and more diverse input. Online collaboration tools can help capture and share stories of success, making it easier to build a repository of positive experiences that can inspire and guide future initiatives.

Another innovative application is to use Appreciative Inquiry in employee onboarding processes. New employees can be introduced to the organization's strengths and successes from the very beginning, helping them feel more connected and aligned with the company's values and goals. This approach can foster a strong sense of belonging and commitment from the outset.

Future initiatives could include creating formal appreciative leadership programs. These programs would train leaders to consistently apply Appreciative Inquiry principles, fostering a leadership style that emphasizes positivity, collaboration, and continuous improvement. Such programs could help cultivate a new generation of leaders who are adept at driving positive change and inspiring their teams.

The appreciative framework can also be extended to customer and client relations. Organizations can engage with their clients using Appreciative Inquiry techniques to understand their positive experiences and expectations better. This approach can enhance customer satisfaction and loyalty by focusing on what clients value most and building stronger, more positive relationships.

For community engagement, organizations can apply Appreciative Inquiry to work with local communities and stakeholders. By identifying and building on community strengths, companies can develop more effective and sustainable corporate social responsibility initiatives. This collaborative approach ensures that community projects are well-received and have a lasting positive impact. In the context of innovation, an appreciative framework can drive a culture of continuous creativity. Organizations can set up innovation labs or think tanks that use Appreciative Inquiry to explore new ideas and solutions. By focusing on past successes and envisioning future possibilities, these labs can generate innovative approaches that propel the organization forward.

Using an appreciative framework in the future involves embedding it into daily operations, leveraging technology, enhancing onboarding processes, developing leadership programs, improving customer relations, engaging with communities, and driving continuous innovation. This approach fosters a positive, collaborative, and forward-thinking organizational environment that supports long-term success and growth.

Chapter 16 has explored the transformative potential of Appreciative Intelligence and Appreciative Inquiry within organizational development. By focusing on recognizing and amplifying strengths, these approaches offer a powerful framework for driving positive change and fostering a culture of continuous improvement and innovation.

Appreciative Intelligence, the ability to see the positive potential in any situation and to act purposefully to realize that potential, is a critical capability for leaders. It empowers individuals and organizations to focus on opportunities rather than obstacles, fostering a proactive and optimistic mindset that drives growth and resilience. Leaders with high Appreciative Intelligence can inspire their teams, cultivate a culture of positivity, and unlock the full potential of their workforce.

The concept of Appreciative Inquiry further enhances this by providing a structured approach to organizational change. By engaging stakeholders in identifying and amplifying what works well, Appreciative Inquiry shifts the focus from problems to possibilities. This collaborative and strength-based process involves the Discovery, Dream, Design, and Destiny phases, guiding organizations through a cycle of positive change. This approach not only leads to more sustainable and impactful outcomes but also builds a more inclusive and collaborative organizational culture.

The applications of Appreciative Inquiry in organizational development are diverse and far-reaching. It can be used in strategic planning, team building, leadership development, culture change initiatives, conflict resolution, and innovation efforts. By consistently applying Appreciative Inquiry principles, organizations can foster a positive, engaged, and forward-thinking environment that supports sustainable growth and success.

Looking to the future, using an appreciative framework opens up numerous possibilities for innovation and growth. Embedding Appreciative Inquiry into daily operations, leveraging technology, enhancing onboarding processes, developing leadership programs, improving customer relations, engaging with communities, and driving continuous creativity are all ways that organizations can continue to evolve and thrive. This approach ensures that organizations remain agile, resilient, and capable of navigating an ever-changing business landscape with confidence and creativity.

As we conclude Chapter 16, it is clear that Appreciative Intelligence and Appreciative Inquiry offer powerful tools for organizational development. By focusing on strengths and possibilities, these approaches foster a culture of positivity, collaboration, and continuous improvement. Let the insights and strategies discussed in this chapter inspire you to integrate Appreciative Intelligence and Inquiry into your organizational practices. By doing so, you can create a thriving, dynamic organization that is well-equipped to achieve long-term success and sustainability. Embrace the power of appreciation to drive meaningful change and unlock new levels of performance and engagement within your organization.

Chapter 17: Dialogic Inquiry and Action Research

In the quest for continuous improvement and meaningful organizational change, Dialogic Inquiry and Action Research emerge as pivotal methodologies. Chapter 17 delves into these two approaches, offering insights into their principles, techniques, and applications within organizations. By fostering open dialogue and iterative learning processes, these methods empower organizations to address complex challenges collaboratively and innovatively.

Dialogic Civility and Inquiry involve engaging in respectful and open-ended conversations that encourage diverse perspectives and foster mutual understanding. This approach emphasizes the importance of creating a safe space for dialogue, where participants feel valued and heard. Dialogic Inquiry is not about winning an argument but about exploring different viewpoints and co-creating knowledge. It promotes critical thinking, empathy, and the collective search for solutions, making it a powerful tool for organizational development and conflict resolution.

Techniques for Dialogic Inquiry include structured dialogues, appreciative conversations, and reflective listening. Structured dialogues provide a framework for discussing specific issues, ensuring that all voices are heard and that the conversation stays focused and productive. Appreciative conversations focus on exploring strengths and successes, helping participants to identify what works well and how to build on it. Reflective listening involves paying close attention to what others are saying, asking clarifying questions, and reflecting back what has been heard to ensure understanding. These techniques create a collaborative environment where new ideas and insights can emerge.

Action Research is a participatory and iterative process that involves diagnosing problems, planning actions, implementing interventions, and evaluating outcomes. It is grounded in the belief that those affected by a problem are best positioned to understand and address it. Action Research combines practical problem-solving with the generation of new knowledge, making it both an approach to change and a research methodology. It is cyclical in nature, with each cycle of action and reflection building on the previous one to create continuous improvement.

Conducting Action Research in organizations involves several key steps. First, a collaborative team is formed, typically comprising members from various levels and departments within the organization. This team works together to identify a problem or area for improvement. Next, the team engages in a thorough diagnosis, gathering data and insights from those affected by the issue. Based on this diagnosis, the team develops a plan of action, outlining specific interventions and strategies to address the problem. These actions are then implemented, with the team closely monitoring progress and gathering feedback. After a set period, the team evaluates the outcomes of their actions, reflecting on what worked well and what could be improved. This reflection informs the next cycle of action, ensuring that the process of learning and improvement continues.

Dialogic Inquiry and Action Research are powerful methodologies for fostering collaborative problem-solving and continuous improvement within organizations. By creating spaces for open dialogue and iterative learning, these approaches enable organizations to address complex challenges in a participatory and innovative manner. This chapter will explore the principles and techniques of Dialogic Inquiry, the process of Action Research, and practical strategies for applying these methods in organizational settings. Let this chapter guide you in harnessing the power of dialogue and action to drive meaningful change and build a dynamic, resilient organization.

Dialogic Civility and Inquiry involve engaging in respectful, open-ended conversations that encourage diverse perspectives and foster mutual understanding. This approach is centered on creating a safe space for dialogue, where participants feel valued and heard. Dialogic Inquiry is not about winning an argument but about exploring different viewpoints and co-creating knowledge. It promotes critical thinking, empathy, and the collective search for solutions. By fostering an environment of respect and openness, Dialogic Civility and Inquiry enable meaningful exchanges that can lead to deeper insights and innovative solutions to complex problems.

In practice, Dialogic Civility means approaching conversations with an attitude of respect and curiosity, genuinely seeking to understand others' perspectives. It requires active listening, where participants pay close attention to what others are saying, ask clarifying questions, and reflect back what has been heard to ensure understanding. This process helps build trust and rapport among participants, which is essential for effective collaboration.

Dialogic Inquiry involves structured dialogues that provide a framework for discussing specific issues, ensuring that all voices are heard and that the conversation remains focused and productive. These dialogues encourage participants to share their experiences, insights, and ideas openly, without fear of judgment or retribution. By focusing on dialogue rather than debate, this approach helps uncover underlying assumptions, reveal new possibilities, and build a shared understanding of the issues at hand.

The goal of Dialogic Civility and Inquiry is to create a collaborative environment where diverse perspectives are valued and collective intelligence is harnessed. This approach recognizes that complex problems often require input from multiple stakeholders and that the best solutions emerge from inclusive and respectful dialogue. By fostering a culture of dialogic inquiry, organizations can enhance their capacity for innovation, adaptability, and continuous improvement.

Techniques for Dialogic Inquiry involve creating structured and supportive environments where meaningful and open-ended conversations can thrive. Structured dialogues provide a framework for discussing specific issues, ensuring that all voices are heard and that the conversation remains focused and productive. This technique helps participants feel comfortable sharing their perspectives and contributes to a more comprehensive understanding of the topic at hand.

Appreciative conversations focus on exploring strengths and successes. By highlighting what works well, participants can identify positive aspects of their experiences and build on them. This approach shifts the focus from problems to possibilities, fostering a positive and proactive mindset. Appreciative conversations help uncover hidden strengths and generate enthusiasm and motivation for future initiatives.

Reflective listening is a crucial component of Dialogic Inquiry. It involves paying close attention to what others are saying, asking clarifying questions, and reflecting back what has been heard to ensure understanding. This technique not only helps verify comprehension but also demonstrates respect and validation for the speaker's contributions. Reflective listening encourages deeper engagement and helps build trust and rapport among participants.

Creating a safe space for dialogue is essential. This means establishing ground rules that promote respect, confidentiality, and openness. Participants should feel assured that their contributions will be valued and that they can speak freely without fear of judgment or retribution. This safe environment is fundamental for honest and meaningful exchanges.

Dialogic Inquiry also benefits from diverse participation. Including individuals from different backgrounds, roles, and perspectives enriches the conversation and ensures a broader range of insights and ideas. Diversity in dialogue fosters creativity and innovation by bringing multiple viewpoints to the table.

Facilitators play a key role in guiding Dialogic Inquiry. Effective facilitators help keep the conversation on track, encourage participation from all members, and ensure that the dialogue remains constructive and focused. They use techniques such as summarizing key points, posing open-ended questions, and managing group dynamics to maintain a productive discussion.

Using visual aids and tools can enhance Dialogic Inquiry. Diagrams, charts, and other visual representations can help clarify complex ideas and facilitate a shared understanding. These tools can also capture and organize the flow of the conversation, making it easier to track progress and revisit important points.

Techniques for Dialogic Inquiry include structured dialogues, appreciative conversations, reflective listening, creating a safe space, encouraging diverse participation, effective facilitation, and using visual aids. These techniques foster an environment of mutual respect and open exploration, enabling participants to engage deeply, share insights, and co-create solutions. By applying these methods, organizations can enhance their capacity for innovation, collaboration, and continuous improvement.

Action Research is a participatory and iterative process that combines practical problem-solving with the generation of new knowledge. It involves a collaborative approach where those affected by a problem are actively involved in diagnosing the issue, planning actions, implementing interventions, and evaluating outcomes. The methodology is cyclical, with each cycle of action and reflection building on the previous one to create continuous improvement.

The core principle of Action Research is that the people experiencing the problem are best positioned to understand and address it. This participatory nature ensures that the interventions are relevant and grounded in the real-world context of the participants. By involving stakeholders throughout the process, Action Research fosters ownership, accountability, and commitment to the change process.

The process begins with identifying a problem or area for improvement. This is followed by a thorough diagnosis, where data is gathered to understand the root causes and context of the issue. Based on this diagnosis, a plan of action is developed, outlining specific interventions and strategies to address the problem. These actions are then implemented, with the team closely monitoring progress and gathering feedback.

After implementation, the outcomes of the actions are evaluated. This evaluation involves reflecting on what worked well and what could be improved. The insights gained from this reflection inform the next cycle of action, allowing for continuous learning and adaptation. This iterative nature of Action Research makes it a powerful tool for driving meaningful and sustainable change.

Action Research is not only a method for solving problems but also a way to generate new knowledge and insights. By systematically documenting the process and outcomes, organizations can develop a deeper understanding of the dynamics at play and contribute to broader knowledge in the field. This dual focus on action and research makes it a valuable approach for both practical and academic endeavors. Action Research is a dynamic and collaborative process that integrates problem-solving with knowledge generation. Its participatory and iterative nature ensures that interventions are relevant, effective, and sustainable, making it a powerful tool for fostering continuous improvement and meaningful change within organizations.

Conducting Action Research in organizations begins with forming a collaborative team composed of members from various levels and departments within the organization. This team works together to identify a problem or area for improvement that is significant to the organization. Engaging diverse stakeholders ensures that the issue is well-understood from multiple perspectives and that the solutions developed will be more comprehensive and effective.

The next step is a thorough diagnosis of the problem. The team gathers data through various methods such as interviews, surveys, observations, and document analysis to understand the root causes and context of the issue. This diagnostic phase is critical as it provides a solid foundation for planning the subsequent actions. Analyzing this data helps to pinpoint specific areas that need intervention and informs the development of a strategic action plan.

Once the problem is clearly defined and understood, the team collaboratively develops a plan of action. This plan outlines specific interventions and strategies aimed at addressing the identified problem. It includes clear objectives, roles and responsibilities, timelines, and resources required. The planning phase ensures that all team members are aligned and that the interventions are feasible and targeted towards achieving the desired outcomes.

The action phase involves implementing the planned interventions. During this phase, the team monitors the progress closely, collecting data and feedback to assess the effectiveness of the actions taken. This real-time monitoring allows for adjustments to be made as needed to ensure that the interventions are on track and addressing the problem effectively.

After a set period, the outcomes of the actions are evaluated. The evaluation phase involves reflecting on the results, analyzing what worked well and what did not, and understanding the impact of the interventions. This reflection is critical for learning and for making informed decisions about the next steps. The insights gained from this evaluation feed into the planning of the next cycle of action, ensuring that the process of improvement is continuous.

The cyclical nature of Action Research, with its repeating phases of planning, action, observation, and reflection, allows organizations to adapt and refine their strategies continually. This iterative process helps in developing a deeper understanding of the organizational dynamics and in creating sustainable solutions to complex problems. By involving stakeholders throughout the process, Action Research fosters a sense of ownership and accountability, which is crucial for the successful implementation of changes.

Conducting Action Research in organizations involves forming a collaborative team, diagnosing the problem through data collection and analysis, developing a strategic action plan, implementing interventions, monitoring progress, evaluating outcomes, and continuously refining the approach based on feedback and reflection. This participatory and iterative methodology enables organizations to address complex challenges effectively and to foster a culture of continuous improvement and learning.

Chapter 17 has delved into the methodologies of Dialogic Inquiry and Action Research, showcasing their vital roles in fostering organizational development and continuous improvement. These approaches emphasize the importance of collaboration, open dialogue, and iterative learning processes to address complex challenges and drive meaningful change.

We began by exploring Dialogic Civility and Inquiry, highlighting the significance of engaging in respectful and open-ended conversations. This method fosters mutual understanding and the co-creation of knowledge by encouraging diverse perspectives and promoting critical thinking. Techniques for Dialogic Inquiry, such as structured dialogues, appreciative conversations, and reflective listening, create an environment where meaningful exchanges can thrive, leading to deeper insights and innovative solutions.

The concept of Action Research was examined next, illustrating its participatory and iterative nature. Action Research combines practical problem-solving with the generation of new knowledge, involving those affected by a problem in diagnosing, planning, implementing, and evaluating interventions. This methodology is cyclical, ensuring continuous improvement through each cycle of action and reflection.

We detailed how to conduct Action Research in organizations, starting with forming a collaborative team and identifying a significant problem. This process involves a thorough diagnosis, developing a strategic action plan, implementing interventions, monitoring progress, and evaluating outcomes. The iterative nature of Action Research allows for continuous learning and adaptation, fostering a culture of resilience and innovation.

The practical applications of these methodologies are extensive. Dialogic Inquiry can enhance team building, leadership development, and conflict resolution by fostering open communication and trust. Action Research, on the other hand, is invaluable for strategic planning, process improvement, and organizational change initiatives, ensuring that interventions are grounded in real-world contexts and stakeholder involvement.

As we conclude Chapter 17, it is clear that Dialogic Inquiry and Action Research offer powerful tools for organizational development. By fostering environments of open dialogue, collaboration, and iterative learning, these methodologies enable organizations to navigate complexities and drive sustainable change. The insights and strategies discussed in this chapter provide a robust framework for leaders and teams to harness the collective intelligence of their organizations, fostering innovation and resilience.

Moving forward, let the principles of Dialogic Inquiry and Action Research inspire you to create a more dynamic and inclusive organizational culture. Embrace the power of open dialogue and iterative learning to address challenges and uncover new opportunities. By integrating these approaches into your organizational practices, you can build a resilient and adaptive organization poised for long-term success and continuous growth.

Chapter 18: Concluding Perspectives on Organizational Development

As we arrive at the final chapter of this book, Chapter 18, we take a moment to reflect on the journey through the rich landscape of organizational development that we have traversed. This concluding chapter aims to review the insights and knowledge gained, summarize the key concepts and practices discussed, and provide reflections on building adaptive and sustainable organizations. Additionally, we will explore future trends in organizational development, offering a forward-looking perspective on where the field is heading.

Throughout this book, we have explored various facets of organizational development, from foundational theories and models to advanced concepts and innovative methodologies. We began by understanding the importance of change management and whole systems thinking, recognizing that successful organizational change requires a comprehensive approach that addresses both the human and systemic aspects of an organization. We delved into core concepts such as diagnostic models, change management strategies, team development, leadership growth, and cultural shaping, emphasizing the importance of these elements in fostering a resilient and dynamic organization.

We also examined the roles of creativity, improvisation, and innovation, highlighting how these factors drive organizational agility and competitiveness. The chapters on social network analysis, micro-level changes, and knowledge management underscored the importance of leveraging relationships, team dynamics, and information flow to enhance organizational performance. Mindfulness and stress reduction techniques were discussed as essential practices for maintaining organizational health and employee well-being.

One of the pivotal themes in this book has been the emphasis on adaptive and resilient organizations. We explored how to design organizations that can swiftly respond to changes and disruptions while maintaining core functions and values. This involved understanding systems dynamics, organizational design principles, and the transition from modern to postmodern and hypermodern workplaces. The integration of Appreciative Intelligence and Inquiry, Dialogic Inquiry, and Action Research provided practical frameworks for fostering a culture of continuous improvement and positive change.

As we summarize the key concepts and practices, it is evident that building adaptive and sustainable organizations requires a holistic and integrated approach. It involves aligning strategy, structure, culture, and processes with the organization's goals and the ever-evolving external environment. This alignment is achieved through continuous learning, innovation, and a commitment to ethical and inclusive practices.

Reflecting on the journey through this book, it is clear that the field of organizational development is dynamic and multifaceted. The principles and methodologies discussed offer valuable tools for leaders and practitioners to navigate the complexities of organizational life. By fostering a culture of adaptability, resilience, and collaboration, organizations can thrive in the face of uncertainty and change.

Looking to the future, several trends are poised to shape the landscape of organizational development. The increasing importance of digital transformation, the growing emphasis on diversity and inclusion, and the need for sustainable business practices are just a few of the factors that will drive the evolution of organizational development. Additionally, the rise of remote work and the ongoing impact of globalization will continue to influence how organizations structure and manage their operations.

As you continue your journey in this field, may the concepts and practices discussed here serve as a guide and inspiration for creating thriving, resilient, and innovative organizations that are well-equipped to navigate the challenges and opportunities of the future.

Throughout this book, we have embarked on an extensive exploration of organizational development, uncovering the various dimensions that contribute to the growth, adaptability, and resilience of modern organizations. Our journey began with the foundational elements of organizational development and change management, emphasizing the critical role these play in navigating the complexities of today's business environment.

We started by understanding the definition and importance of organizational development (OD) and change management. These concepts are pivotal for guiding organizations through transitions and ensuring that changes are implemented smoothly and successfully. The historical evolution of OD provided context, tracing its roots from early 20th-century scientific management to contemporary approaches that emphasize human factors and holistic systems thinking.

Core concepts and approaches in OD were examined in depth, including diagnostic models and tools, change management strategies, team development, leadership development, and shaping organizational culture. These elements form the backbone of effective organizational development, enabling organizations to diagnose issues accurately, implement strategic changes, and foster a positive and productive work environment.

We then delved into the role of creativity, improvisation, and innovation, exploring how these aspects drive organizational agility and competitiveness. The importance of fostering a culture that encourages creative problem-solving and innovative thinking was highlighted, with practical examples demonstrating the benefits of these approaches.

Chapters on social network analysis, micro-level changes, and knowledge management emphasized the importance of leveraging relationships, team dynamics, and information flow. By understanding and optimizing these areas, organizations can enhance communication, collaboration, and overall performance.

Mindfulness and stress reduction techniques were also discussed, recognizing their essential role in maintaining organizational health and employee well-being. These practices help create a supportive work environment that promotes mental and emotional resilience, enabling employees to thrive.

The concept of designing adaptive and resilient organizations was a central theme, focusing on systems dynamics, organizational design principles, and the transition from modern to postmodern and hypermodern workplaces. We explored how organizations can develop structures and processes that allow them to respond swiftly to changes and disruptions while maintaining core functions and values.

Appreciative Intelligence and Inquiry, along with Dialogic Inquiry and Action Research, provided practical frameworks for fostering a culture of continuous improvement and positive change. These methodologies emphasize the importance of engaging stakeholders, leveraging strengths, and promoting open dialogue to drive meaningful and sustainable organizational development.

As we reflect on these key learnings, it becomes evident that building adaptive and sustainable organizations requires a holistic and integrated approach. Aligning strategy, structure, culture, and processes with organizational goals and the external environment is crucial. This alignment is achieved through continuous learning, innovation, and a commitment to ethical and inclusive practices.

Looking ahead, several trends are poised to shape the future of organizational development. Digital transformation will continue to be a significant driver, necessitating the adoption of new technologies and digital strategies. The emphasis on diversity, equity, and inclusion will grow, as organizations recognize the value of diverse perspectives and inclusive practices in driving innovation and performance. Sustainable business practices will also become increasingly important, as organizations respond to environmental challenges and societal expectations.

Remote work and globalization will further influence organizational structures and management practices, requiring flexible and adaptive approaches. The integration of advanced analytics and artificial intelligence will offer new opportunities for optimizing organizational processes and decision-making.

Organizational development (OD) involves a systematic approach to improving an organization's effectiveness and capacity to change. Change management focuses on guiding organizations through transitions to achieve desired outcomes. Both concepts are essential for navigating today's complex and dynamic business environments. The field of OD has evolved from early scientific management principles, emphasizing efficiency and task optimization, to contemporary approaches that prioritize human factors, systems thinking, and holistic change strategies.

Key elements of OD include diagnostic models and tools, which help organizations assess their current state and identify areas for improvement. Change management strategies guide the implementation of changes, ensuring they are adopted smoothly and sustainably. Team development focuses on enhancing team dynamics and performance, while leadership development nurtures leaders who can drive change and inspire their teams. Shaping organizational culture involves creating an environment that supports the organization's values and goals.

Fostering a culture of creativity and innovation is critical for organizational agility and competitiveness. Encouraging creative problem-solving and improvisation helps organizations adapt to changes and seize new opportunities. Case studies of innovation through improvisation demonstrate the practical benefits of these approaches.

Understanding and leveraging social networks within an organization can enhance communication, collaboration, and innovation. Tools and methods for social network analysis help identify key influencers, communication patterns, and opportunities for improving information flow and connectivity.

Enhancing team dynamics through effective communication, collaboration, and leveraging team strengths is crucial for organizational success. Recognizing and rewarding team performance fosters a positive and productive work environment.

Effective knowledge management strategies facilitate the creation, sharing, and utilization of knowledge within an organization. The role of technology in knowledge management is significant, enabling efficient information storage, retrieval, and dissemination. Building a knowledge-sharing culture encourages continuous learning and innovation.

Incorporating mindfulness and stress reduction techniques into organizational practices promotes mental and emotional well-being, enhancing overall organizational health. These practices help employees manage stress, stay focused, and maintain a positive outlook.

Adaptive organizations can respond swiftly to changes and disruptions, while resilient organizations can withstand shocks and maintain core functions. Principles of systems dynamics and organizational design, along with the transition to postmodern and hypermodern workplaces, are essential for building such organizations.

Appreciative Intelligence involves recognizing and realizing positive potential, while Appreciative Inquiry focuses on identifying and amplifying strengths within an organization. These approaches foster a positive, collaborative, and innovative culture.

Dialogic Inquiry involves engaging in respectful and open-ended conversations to explore diverse perspectives and co-create knowledge. Action Research is a participatory and iterative process that combines problem-solving with knowledge generation, fostering continuous improvement and meaningful change.

The future of OD will be shaped by digital transformation, the emphasis on diversity, equity, and inclusion, and the need for sustainable business practices. Remote work, globalization, advanced analytics, and artificial intelligence will also influence organizational structures and management practices.

By understanding and applying these key concepts and practices, leaders and practitioners can create dynamic, resilient, and innovative organizations that are well-equipped to navigate the challenges and opportunities of the future. This holistic and integrated approach to organizational development ensures long-term success and sustainability.

Building adaptive and sustainable organizations requires a holistic and forward-thinking approach that integrates various elements of organizational development. Reflecting on the journey through this book, several key insights emerge about what it takes to create such organizations.

At the core of building adaptive and sustainable organizations is the ability to embrace change and foster a culture of continuous learning and improvement. Organizations must develop the capacity to respond swiftly to changing environments, seize new opportunities, and navigate uncertainties. This adaptability is achieved through fostering a mindset that values innovation, creativity, and resilience.

The role of leadership is paramount in driving adaptability and sustainability. Leaders must be visionary, inspiring, and capable of guiding their teams through transitions with confidence and clarity. They need to cultivate an environment where employees feel empowered to experiment, take risks, and learn from failures. By modeling these behaviors themselves, leaders can set the tone for a culture that embraces change and values continuous growth.

Creating a positive organizational culture that supports adaptability and sustainability involves promoting inclusivity, collaboration, and open communication. Employees should feel valued and heard, with their diverse perspectives contributing to the collective intelligence of the organization. This inclusive culture not only enhances engagement and morale but also drives innovation by bringing a wide range of ideas and solutions to the table.

Effective knowledge management is another critical component. Organizations must facilitate the creation, sharing, and utilization of knowledge to ensure that valuable insights are accessible to those who need them. Leveraging technology to enhance knowledge management processes can significantly improve efficiency and innovation. Building a culture that encourages knowledge sharing and continuous learning helps organizations stay ahead of the curve and maintain a competitive edge.

The principles of systems thinking and organizational design play a vital role in building adaptive and sustainable organizations. Understanding the interconnections within the organization and the broader environment allows for more effective decision-making and strategic planning. Designing flexible structures and processes that can be reconfigured as needed enables organizations to adapt quickly to changes and disruptions.

Incorporating mindfulness and stress reduction techniques into organizational practices is essential for maintaining the well-being of employees. A healthy workforce is more resilient and better equipped to handle challenges. Promoting mental and emotional well-being helps create a supportive environment where employees can thrive and contribute their best work.

Sustainability also involves a commitment to ethical practices and social responsibility. Organizations must consider the long-term impact of their actions on the environment and society. By integrating sustainability into their core values and operations, organizations can build trust with stakeholders and ensure their long-term viability.

As we look to the future, the trends shaping organizational development will continue to evolve. Digital transformation, the growing emphasis on diversity and inclusion, and the need for sustainable business practices will drive the evolution of organizations. Embracing these trends and integrating them into the organizational fabric will be crucial for staying relevant and competitive.

Reflecting on building adaptive and sustainable organizations highlights the importance of embracing change, fostering a culture of continuous learning and improvement, effective leadership, positive organizational culture, knowledge management, systems thinking, employee well-being, and ethical practices. By integrating these elements, organizations can create a dynamic, resilient, and sustainable environment that is well-equipped to navigate the challenges and opportunities of the future.

As we look towards the future, several emerging trends are poised to shape the field of organizational development. Understanding and integrating these trends will be essential for organizations seeking to remain competitive and innovative in an increasingly complex and dynamic environment.

Digital transformation continues to revolutionize how organizations operate. Digital tools and platforms are enhancing communication, collaboration, and decision-making processes. Artificial intelligence, machine learning, and data analytics are providing deeper insights into organizational performance and customer behavior. Embracing digital transformation allows organizations to streamline operations, improve efficiency, and foster innovation.

The importance of diversity, equity, and inclusion (DEI) in the workplace is gaining greater recognition. Organizations are increasingly focused on creating inclusive cultures that value diverse perspectives and ensure equitable opportunities for all employees. DEI initiatives not only enhance employee engagement and satisfaction but also drive creativity and better decision-making. Future organizational development strategies will need to prioritize DEI to attract and retain top talent and to reflect the values of an increasingly diverse global market.

Environmental sustainability and social responsibility are becoming critical components of organizational strategy. Organizations are expected to reduce their environmental footprint, adopt sustainable practices, and contribute positively to society. This shift is driven by stakeholder expectations, regulatory requirements, and a growing awareness of the impact of business on the planet. Sustainable practices are not only good for the environment but also enhance brand reputation and long-term viability.

The COVID-19 pandemic has accelerated the adoption of remote work, demonstrating its viability and benefits. As a result, many organizations are transitioning to hybrid work models that combine remote and in-office work. This flexibility can improve work-life balance, reduce overhead costs, and expand the talent pool by allowing organizations to hire from a broader geographic area. Organizational development will need to address the challenges and opportunities of managing distributed teams and maintaining a cohesive culture in a hybrid work environment.

The pace of change in the business world requires a commitment to lifelong learning. Organizations must invest in continuous learning and development to keep their workforce skilled and adaptable. This includes upskilling and reskilling employees to meet the demands of new technologies and changing market conditions. Creating a culture that supports ongoing education and professional growth will be crucial for maintaining a competitive edge.

The ability to quickly adapt to change and recover from disruptions is more important than ever. Organizations that prioritize agility and resilience can better navigate uncertainties and capitalize on emerging opportunities. This involves fostering a culture of innovation, implementing flexible structures and processes, and developing strategic foresight to anticipate and respond to changes in the environment.

As you embark on your journey in organizational development, remember that the landscape will continue to evolve. Embrace these trends and integrate them into your strategies and practices. Stay curious, open to learning, and willing to adapt. The insights and tools provided in this book are meant to guide you, but your unique experiences and perspectives will shape your path.

Good luck on your journey to fostering dynamic, resilient, and innovative organizations. May you find success in creating environments where people and businesses can thrive, and may your efforts contribute to a better, more sustainable future for all.

www.ingramcontent.com/pod-product-compliance
Lightning Source LLC
Chambersburg PA
CBHW050209230526
45470CB00001B/307